IN EXTREMIS

ESSAYS

❧

JAKE GOLDSMITH

Sagging
Meniscus

Set in Trump Mediaeval with LATEX.

ISBN: 978-1-963846-45-4 (paperback)
ISBN: 978-1-963846-46-1 (ebook)
Library of Congress Control Number: 2025943199

Sagging Meniscus Press
Montclair, New Jersey
saggingmeniscus.com

For Wendy and Kooper

I write entirely to find out what I'm thinking, what I'm looking at, what I see and what it means. What I want and what I fear.

—Joan Didion, *Why I Write (1976)*

And therefore, Reader, I myself am the subject of my book: it is not reasonable that you should employ your leisure on a topic so frivolous and vain. Therefore, Farewell.

—Michel de Montaigne

I still have a "dire need" to write, but even at times of oppressive doubts about myself, about everyone and everything, I remain certain that creative work not only can mean steadily evolving freedom for an individual but also helps to preserve and augment freedom in the world.

—Manès Sperber, *Until My Eyes Are Closed with Shards*

If ever I reach old age; and if one day, still pondering many thoughts, but turning from speech with men, I have near me a friend to receive my last farewell, let my chair be set on the short grass, with the peaceful daises before me, beneath the sun and far-spread sky, so that in the act of quitting this fleeting life, I may recover some touch of the infinite illusion.

—Étienne Pivert de Senancour, *Obermann*

CONTENTS

This collection of brief essays was written quickly, or hastily, over the last months of 2024 and the beginning of 2025, intended for the literary magazine *Exacting Clam*. It is a work of unprofessional scholarship or a *personal exegesis*, meant to translate thoughts onto a page instead of irking me while stuck inside my head. However flawed, they are an honest attempt at self-expression; something that may justifiably reveal my essential impulse or inner necessity. Moreover, there's the morose idea I've elucidated sufficiently in my memoir or previous essays: how I feel a physiological urgency to have a say, even if it is deeply indulgent and self-interested, before I can't anymore due to the progression of illness. It at once gives me a confidence to speak while also feeling desperate or pathetic. It is hardly about broad recognition, but the fact remains: a physical book is a material imprint on the world that may actually be more durable than a digital blog or ephemeral social media post. Software is liable to deletion and web servers need power — a book has to survive the elements and in 100 years, someone will still likely be able to read a book where some old blog may well die in 10 after the web hosting is kaput. Digitising something to preserve it is a useful trick, but it is a subtle lie to say that the digital world is inherently more permanent and not vulnerable to the deterioration of hardware. After too many reservations I can't accept it as selfish or malignly egotistic to want to leave some faint imprint on the world.

Beyond the number of intellectual influences anyone absorbs via osmosis, much as Wittgenstein said—"it is indifferent to me whether what I have thought has already been thought before me by another" (while I'm hopefully more grateful), I should at least acutely acknowledge P.J. Blumenthal, David Collard, William Fear, my publishers at Sagging Meniscus Press, Wendy Shanel Behrend and Kooper Wilson for their aid in either reading or providing the opportunity for my disparate thoughts to exist in print.

Jake Goldsmith, February 2025

IN EXTREMIS

AUTISTIC LIBERALISM

CONFUSED MEANINGS AND DEFINITIONS

EFINITIONS of liberalism are deeply confused—a word, idea, or set of ideas, used in every sense and soon lacking any sense at all. Overuse and confusion can apply to any philosophical idea, political implementation, or popular ideology, but I want to draw particular attention to liberalism and its misuse (without providing a dogmatic definition), rather than socialism, conservatism, etc., all with their own particular follies and all frequently misunderstood.

I risk being rude or intellectually primitive, but I fail to see a consistent or reliable definition of liberalism, in all its varieties, outside niche academic circles. Although it is not really the scope of this piece to provide a comprehensive explanation, liberalism, considered only as a concept, let alone a physical and infrastructural reality, appears more malleable and easily subverted or self-subverted in its motifs or its intentions, than other historical or contemporary political ideas applied to reality. I won't attempt to give some perfect definition here (if that is even possible). And indeed, there are certainly varieties of liberalism that I reject. There are versions of liberalism less hospitable to democracy, noting the strong possibility that wider democratic participation can be reactionary rather than constructive or helpful—which is still in some part an inherent fragility democratic regimes must contend with. Hopefully I can justify my ambivalence to dogmatic definitions later. I want to at least suggest, briefly, an outline of the particular meanings of liberal thought, its inherent vulnerability, and a rejection of varied positivist notions of liberalism and other ideologies. If I detailed every instance of the use of liberalism as a label (many of which are inaccurate or absurd) I could write several volumes, for which reason I only want to write a brief outline of a particular understanding, sharing an ambivalent view of historical epistemology with Raymond Aron and his *Introduction à la philoso-*

phie de l'histoire (*Introduction to the Philosophy of History–1938*).

Part of this analysis is likely impoverished given my particular reading, and my rejection of popular, contemporary analyses of liberalism in its multiplicity of meanings, analyses of so-called post-liberalism, and a possibly *autistic* focus on history and historical motifs (in short, ideals) with the view that many liberal governments are only nominally liberal; suffering from democratic degeneration and abuses of power that undermine them. I want to avoid common talk where political categories are used pejoratively—and whether one is rightly opposed to something or not, there is little understanding of what any category is or should be. There's often talk in semi-scholarly literature, or more rudely on the internet, of the death of liberalism or of other ideologies. These declarations should be proposed with more acute and deliberate meanings, but often give us obtuse or misleading, contradictory meanings instead. All such meanings and definitions have very personal, individual understandings behind them—political names can be regarded as anything the author wants them to mean without much diligence, depending more on aesthetic dispositions. These often basic or abstract definitions make polemics and critique much easier. Shallow versions of the left, or the centre, or the right can shape language in any fashion—with language being better at describing dreams and emotions than considered thought. It matters if we have silly or outright wrong understandings of what political ideologies are even if we dislike them. How is one meant to be better, or combat what is worse, if we don't attempt to have more cogent (if never perfect) definitions? Many are immune to such teachings no matter what the source, having already made up their minds and become resistant to information. But we have to live with this tension.

Instead of holding consistent aspirations, regimes as well as personal ideas need to be understood as inconsistent and hypocritical. "People have always created history in the name of ideas, but the history they have created has never faithfully reflected their ideas", as Aron said. Some ideas can easily lend themselves to bad interpretations. Simply providing a dictionary would be somewhat of an improvement to reducing misunderstandings, but never sufficiently robust. As a brief example, *economic liberalism* has many dissimilarities, or is antithetical, to liberalism as defined in other senses. Hayek and Keynes, or 21st century wealth speculation and the oft-forgotten social concerns of Adam Smith, have a great many differences and are considerably at odds with each other. The decline of social liberalism in the name of runaway economic interest is often lamentable, with its results often very *illiberal* and just as inhumanly bureaucratic as maligned systems of central planning.

THE INHERENT FRAGILITY OF LIBERAL DEMOCRACY

John Adams said: ". . . democracy never lasts long. It soon wastes, exhausts, and murders itself. There never was a democracy yet that did not commit suicide."

The full quote provides greater pessimism. Since Adams, our liberal democracies, whatever their sins, have had more success and have proved surprisingly resilient. But this lesson, one of an inherent vulnerability, is one we shouldn't forget. Today we risk the degeneration of liberal democracies (nominal or not) for many reasons: through corruption, anti-democratic policies, a crisis of trust in institutions, unregulated technologies, a neo-feudalistic organisation of wealth, the meddling of foreign enemies, and our own weaknesses and irresponsibility.

In the realm of theory, and not only in practice, something integral to liberalism easily undermines it. Broad ideas of conservatism, socialism, communism, monarchism, or fascism, in the realm of theory and intention or in their physical infrastructure, all provide, one might cautiously say, greater *tolerances* or leeway for moral or political aberrations while maintaining themselves. I'm approaching a 'No True Scotsman' notion of political and philosophical concepts which can easily be regarded as cheap. A socialist regime, or a socially and culturally conservative regime, allows for a greater breadth of policy and *illiberal* behaviour without ceasing to be *socialist* or *conservative*. These regimes, or more abstract ideas, can subvert themselves in other ways so that they may not be considered authentic anymore, but the contention here is that it is far easier, due to the constitutive parts of what liberalism should be, for liberalism and liberal democracy to become corrupted and *no longer liberal*. Meaning: it is a far more fragile idea. I think this may be the case, in analysis, whether I am favourable or not to liberalism—while my particular understanding of it is idiosyncratic and likely open to derision.

The separation of powers is not just a safeguard against abuse, but contingent on liberty itself—which cannot exist if not delicately balanced and precariously mediated. Do other regimes care so much about this, or do they require such an easily corrupted balance? Some might, unfortunately, care less about being delicate mediators. Democracy faces the same challenge—a balance which most governments have achieved only imperfectly and are always susceptible to ruin.

THE TENUOUS RELATIONSHIP BETWEEN IDEAS AND PRACTICE

The failures of Stalinism are often regarded as clear failures to correctly interpret inspiring ideas. I would say this is partly—and reasonably—true, but not absolutely true. Contemporaries of Marx, on the Left or otherwise, warned of possible and easy interpretations of Marxist thought that could lead to catastrophe. Kołakowski also proposed this view. It is true and almost obvious that there isn't some direct line from Marx to Stalin (as if Marx ever wanted the USSR). It is rather that though Marx isn't guilty of what came after him he was in some part responsible by proclaiming prophetic ideas that lend them-

selves readily to despotism or demagoguery—an unfortunate legacy that was closer to predictable than
impossible. Marx was a genius, and a genius economic diagnostician, but as a prophet and moralis-
ing historicist his legacy is wearying. It may be more
difficult to make the case that the ideas of Montesquieu and Tocqueville would bear such sour fruit;
while we cannot discount the possibility that they
do. The failures of liberalism or of liberal democracy are not failures of Montesquieu's disposition or
motifs, if we are being charitable. Further credence
could be given to this idea in that Montesquieu did
not offer any utopian visions which soon succumb
to prejudice, while others enthusiastically did. It is
harder to corrupt cautious warnings of what *might*
happen than active calls to change history as part of
grand schemes.

The failures of descendent actions are more
likely to be at odds with historical intention or
ideal intention. I could suggest, much like 19th
century abolitionists, that broadly understood Enlightenment ideas of liberty and equality aren't
so much bad in themselves; the failure is in that
they're inconsistently, hypocritically, and too narrowly applied—that their proponents don't follow
their espoused ideas to the letter, or we still haven't

found a proper application, if that's ever possible. It is likewise true that overconfidence, or a pseudoscientific justification of one's apparent truth or correctness, can lead to the justification of all sorts of bad behaviour; and historical or contemporary liberals can still easily believe in such outmoded *scientific* and *natural* justifications as much as political Hegelians or Marxists. With any idea, or any proponent of an idea, we must be wary of latent assumptions and historical epistemology. I will not be bold and say that there could ever be a thing like a perfected liberalism where broad ideas of tolerance, civility, liberty, or equality are not perverted by reality, especially given various diffuse weaknesses. An overemphasis on *individualism*, privatisation, deregulation, has produced callous disregard for vulnerable people and neglect for the basic maintenance of public services. Many so-called liberals have enacted hierarchical, even authoritarian, and abusive policies that reek of clear hypocrisy.

Eugenics has been justified as a progressive measure despite its, frankly, evil and fascistic constitution. Fair ideals even with a fairer implementation can still cause unintended consequences and uncomfortable trade-offs, while it is arguably the case that the flaws of liberal democracies are more often instances of *illiberal* behaviour — or egalitarianism, liberty, and justice denied, unachieved, or adulterated by unjust passions or industrial progress. Industrial and technological progress, and the hierarchies they necessitate, produce an unease with equitable principles that might be impossible to soothe, or is at least exhaustingly difficult to mitigate. Other societies, or governments, have less of a problem here—if, in the pursuit of technological or economic progress, one has fewer misgivings with societal unease and injustice.

There is still something of an *unbridgeable gap* between the memory of past decisions and present-day experiences. With that said, I will be bold in saying the failures of other non-liberal regimes and their infrastructure may, more likely, have a closer but certainly not straightforward relationship to originating ideas. Such gaps between ideas and practice are always present, but not always the same length.

> Specialists are aware of an economist named Marx, richer, more subtle, and more interesting than the author only of *Capital*. But the useful Marx, so to speak, the one who may have changed the history of the world, is the one who propagated false ideas . . .

> ... As an economist, Marx remains perhaps
> the richest, the most exciting of his time. As
> an economist-prophet, as a putative ancestor of
> Marxism-Leninism, he is an accursed sophist
> who bears some responsibility for the horrors
> of the twentieth century.

—Raymond Aron, *Memoirs*

TELEOLOGY, PHILOSOPHY, AND HISTORY

Whether it is invoked pejoratively, especially when we regard the crimes and mistakes of contemporary *neoliberalism*, or defined favourably, it is difficult to say liberalism, or the broadest understanding of an egalitarian ideal, has been truly achieved. Is this an audacious statement? The thinker I am most fond of, Raymond Aron, is atypical of some negative or positive understandings of liberalism, especially after his death, and it is easy for me to contend that so-called liberal democracies, especially since the 1980s and 1990s, have not heeded Aronian warnings of their own vulnerability and the possibility of decline. Like Aron I don't find easy comfort in any political orthodoxy, and I am endlessly critical of liberal regimes, while I don't accept their enemies. The further development of neoliberal ideas in the post-Soviet era has suffered similar mistakes to past so-

cialist ideas: a type of teleological arrogance. Meaning, an implicit Fukuyama-esque notion—that their
ideas, given a false confidence after the fall of their
rival, have the vibe of historical inevitability, narra-
tological victory, or obviousness.

We shouldn't blame Francis Fukuyama so much
individually for the supposed inaccuracy of his
ideas, or *strawman* him (it is not as if he is some
primary influence on world governments), but we
can note the lamentable techno-optimism to which
he gave a more acute and explicit expression. The
so-called and much derided 'End of History' (of
the post-1989 order), with a misplaced optimism
about its own health and underestimation of anti-
democratic forces, is foolhardy. That is in no way an
original critique, but continued criticism of these
attitudes, well-defined or ill-defined, is warranted.
What's known as *reactionary*, or populist, is not
some aberration but a consequence of neoliberal
hubris—even if its thinking and its methods are a
foolish and counterproductive way to react to such
arrogance. Democratic degeneration, or illiberal beliefs and policy, result from the weaknesses, crimes,
and mistakes of nominally democratic regimes—
not only from nefarious foreign interventions or
outside prejudice. This doesn't mean we must fear

total democratic collapse, but we should be watchful of such degradation and take responsibility for our own weaknesses.

Truthfully I'm not here to defend liberalism *per se* but a particular instance of it. I regard *teleological* liberalism, or a positivist liberalism, or the thought that a philosophy or political approach has a metaphysical, divine, mechanical, spiritual, or natural inclination to becoming dominant . . . as foolish, incorrect, and just as incorrect whether one supposes history has a goal in socialism, or progress, or any political *ism*. I am ambivalent in my idea of history, or the history of ideas, as I am ambivalent towards the above in any human nature. There are no sure political aims inherent in human nature, while there may be sure vices that favour some forms of societal organisation more than others, and there is *no automatic selection* (of political ideas and regimes) *which conforms with our moral requirements.*

Concepts such as reason, progress, or the basic adherence to facts and truth, are theoretical possibilities, and we are ill-equipped in their application to prevent tragedy or otherwise ensure moral or technical progress. They are not intrinsic, they won't be automatically or organically victorious, and despite various sophisticated objections many still be-

lieve, emotionally, in a universe bent towards justice or progress. Some liberals suggest humans are
inherently rational, presenting an idealistic concept
of human motives that remains abstract and easily eroded. One can't be naively optimistic about
human vices. Ideologies need to contend with people being irrational or emotional. La Rochefoucauld
should remind us: we often lack the strength to follow reason fully, and we are tremendously unreasonable. Ignorance, or stupidity, very much play a role
in history and political action. I cannot say progress
is impossible, I do not, and I certainly do want pro-
gressions in justice and equity. Yet it is still the case
given human freedom or the unpredictability of future existence that we cannot say progress is obvious, natural, or probable; and I'm prone to being
pessimistic. A truer philosophy of history allows us
fewer settled convictions.

Many sorts of liberals, neoliberals, anarchists
of various stripes, communists, conservatives, free
market libertarians, popular right-wing insurrec-
tionists, and fascists reject the above in some way—
they can be inclined to a belief in their own exis-
tential superiority and the certain, even axiomatic
quality of their plans. They can be too confident
in their justifications of themselves and in their

understanding of their opponents. Of course some may be more modest, or truthful, and not believe that their ideas are so clearly justified, whatever they are—but I'd contend that many still suppose their view of reality, their philosophy, their ideology, is obvious, *common sense*, or evidently true— and that it should be obvious to others. This entails a few things, I think: a mistaken assumption on the workings of history, the scope of human rationality, the inept conveyance of perceived better ideas, a sense of what is contingent, and a false sense of how one's own ideas (or antagonistic ideas) proliferate or are soon rejected. I can think I have good ideas, or maybe know what's in our better interest (or at least mine), but this does not mean my views are popular, self-evident, achievable, and that common incentives mean things I'm opposed to don't have an easier time getting their way. I don't suppose humans are inherently good either; we are more likely to gratify our passions, and it requires an exhaustingly difficult process to incentivise better behaviour without resulting in tyranny or anarchy.

> . . . the liberal believes in the permanence of humanity's imperfection, he resigns himself to a regime in which the good will be the result of numberless actions, and never the object of a conscious choice. Finally, he subscribes to the pes-

simism that sees, in politics, the art of creating
the conditions in which the vices of men will contribute to the good of the state.

—Raymond Aron, *The Opium of The Intellectuals*

This is opposed to a sometimes-liberal conceit
that moral persuasion and an inherent goodness in
humanity can promote a broadly humanistic, rational and free society. I suppose that some varieties
of progress and justice are genuine, and I reasonably do not disagree with righteous diagnoses of our
moral and societal failures. The ideas and applications of progress, freedom, justice, equality are all
a grinding affair, a difficult marathon, easily ruined,
readily degraded, while a mediocre performance being the least bad possibility is immediately aesthetically unpopular today just as it was in the 1950s
or around the publication of Aron's *Introduction à
la philosophie de l'histoire*, or in antiquity. We may
resonate more with impatient demands. Technological progress reveals greater moral failures, as moral
justice does not follow so soon from industrial prosperity. We are rightly disillusioned and justly not
content with our lot, with continued abuse, with a
type of hopeless resignation to injustice and a slow
crawl that may quickly be halted or reversed. We

demand more and it is no doubt good to dream of better futures. These are noble wishes.

What's still eternally of concern is what John Milton called "the known rules of ancient liberty". This does not mean we are resigned to a slow and hollow Burkeanism. The socialist Proudhon, the liberal Tocqueville, and Karl Marx were all severe in their criticisms of the *imitators* of the Great Revolution, 'the comedians of 1848'. Mary Wollstonecraft, whose ideas we take for granted, knew the dangers of revolt much like others. The fight for liberty doesn't presume morality or good politics. To use another famous expression, it is one of the easiest and most regrettable processes for revolt and revolution, in the name of good causes or not, to be hoisted by its own petard. Pessimism becomes more reasonable, while we are hopefully not resigned to it. Strategy and good tactics are alien concepts to many revolutionaries. What miraculous formula is there that could rid us of our inequalities? This isn't some cheap question. It is easy for some to honestly answer, but this doesn't suppose intelligible, let alone politicised, ways of achieving it. I'm sorry for being doubtful; I'd much rather have fewer doubts and it is still much worth it, after all this caution, for people to optimistically dream.

CONCLUSION

While I am not bold enough to suggest what will surely work—equivocation is sort of the point—this doesn't suppose anyone else, even if guilty of their own failures, can't analyse vital flaws in others.

With all this I've likely failed to give a distilled, clearer definition of a better societal organisation; nor, probably, have I cleared up the confusion around the multiplicity of definitions for liberalism. I've mostly made negative suggestions against a type of historicism or teleological ideology that is not unique to varieties of liberalism, with the vague hope against the odds that others might do better. We do better if we know the fragility of espoused ideological principles, and we do better if we know the confusing differences between ideas and their practice, and yet . . . If equivocation is an intellectual strength in some regard, then it is easily a practical weakness in others. How is an idea that's inherently equivocal supposed to succeed? I doubt the equivocating and pluralistic ideas I align with, or share with the likes of Aron, will have an easy time finding a good application to modern society or finding much influence. I can rightly critique the wrongdoing of any sort of doctrinaire ideology, but that doesn't mean such critiques will lead to (physical) success—even if they are more astute, more sophisticated, and more aware of the failures of past regimes. I'm bad at pretending to be a scholar and it is easy for me to cheap-out and direct a reader to others with far more depth, breadth, and precision in their analysis. Laziness doesn't help either. I at least hope that I have hinted at an importance in different meanings, a keener (while imperfect) awareness of philosophical underpinnings, and it is still a good affirmation to note the foolishness and dishonesty of overly-teleological ideas.

Liberalism, in its better iterations, is constitutively pluralistic and conscious of history; and so, if we want to be more truthful and consistent, this requires less dogmatism and more fluidity—which is both positive and negative. It is much more difficult, I think, to have a settled orthodoxy that is 'liberal' than a settled orthodoxy that is not: it is more constitutively vulnerable than other influences. A clear orthodoxy is often regarded as helpful, but as I hope I have detailed, an apparently righteous historicism, be it socialist, liberal, capitalist, conservative, or otherwise, can predictably lead to demagoguery, crimes, and failure. Caution, prudence, or wariness about optimistic and utopian aims mean we may be less likely to produce prejudicial results—although what negatives we tolerate or the capacity to remain in power is another matter.

Political ideas of the same name can prove vastly different depending on prior psychology, persuasive limits, humility, or one's epistemology of history. If one wants a better understanding of politics, then it helps to navigate the diversity of meanings, even if one rejects my analysis of liberal thought—especially given, as I'll always admit, the easily perceptible failures and hypocrisy of modern liberal regimes. People should not, I hope, become too comfortable and confident in what they perceive as possible. The dim dream of a better world requires diligence and prudence just as much as it may require courage and impatience, lest so much effort result in ruin.

I doubt the above is very persuasive. The best result would be to accept something of what I've said here—though I'm mostly a conduit for others—and then prove me wrong.

Autumn 2024

ON CONSERVATION

W HAT does it mean to *conserve*? Across the entire ideological spectrum there is talk of conserving and preserving land, nature, culture, and history. There's little considered thought about what that means, and all the bitter ironies. Walking through old buildings I feel conflicting impulses. One is what I'd glibly call *Goethe's Feeling*, trying to find a real and compelling connection to ancient history among silent architecture—though I'm not in Rome:

> *Tell me you stones, O speak, you towering palaces!*
> *Streets, say a word! Spirit of this place, are you dumb?*
> *All things are alive in your sacred walls*
> *eternal Ipswich, only for me all's still.*

Chaucer lived in Ipswich. But going to Ipswich today you may experience a local form of Paris Syndrome, as is the case in over-expectant Asian tourists: despair at the dirt and grime of modern Britain, with just a thin haunted shadow of history hiding around dark corners near Betfred and a dozen phone repair-cum-vape emporiums. Another impulse is *conservative*, in the older, perhaps better meaning of the word — pastoral, nurturing, rural, wanting to preserve deteriorating architecture and dying nature rather than lower taxes and build a mega pork and chicken factory near King's Lynn, polluting nearby rivers or squashing badgers in my brand-new BMW. It becomes increasingly difficult to feel something; something the heathen me can never call spiritual, in ancient spaces and in pretty landscapes. I want to preserve churches but I don't want, or need, some comforting myth to make my sentimentality worth more. It is rude to suggest that only the God-bothering can *really* have a true and deeper connection with the past, with the stones, with life, as if the intensity of their conceit, so fantastical, maybe approaching delusion, can be an intense gratification and justification for wanting nice things, rather than anything perverse. I don't need to believe in any elevated metaphysics or theological dogma to recognise a good building and a good story.

Occasionally I do feel something, but it is more about the prospect of losing things. It would be a deep shame to demolish a thousand year old building (disregarding any listed status), in disuse or not, or replace some other landscape, to build an identikit housing estate. This appears very obvious, although I am no so-called *nimby*. I would very much like the propagation of more housing, and better housing, though there's a question of not, in Ruskin's words, producing such "comfortless and unhonoured dwellings", and it is insulting to think that we somehow cannot do this; when we are otherwise so abundant and wealthy.

It is difficult for me to walk far. Illness restricts my ability to wander through forests and picturesque countryside, so any experience of the rolling hills of Suffolk is rarer, more precious, less common or boring. Countryside is worth a lot and is easy to lose. It takes more effort to repair it and sustain it.

Much of the modern world is so quickened, so hastily built up and torn down again in destructive renewal. We often mock Americans for having little history or no old buildings. Americans mock them-

selves for this; Americans visiting Britain marvel
at quaint brick cottages and structures older than
nations... But America does have history, and has
known beauty in the sort of dated pre-modern architecture many of us love: particularly civic architecture. The United States produced some of
the grandest and most beautiful train stations to
ever exist. They destroyed them. There's always
an irony to what we call *conservatism*: the histo-
rian J. G. A. Pocock asked American conservatives
what was it of their culture they wanted to conserve? They do no good job at conserving much at
all, and are far better at societal arson and insur-

rections. America is a land of radical destruction before much else. The most vocal self-proclaimed modern conservatives have no motivation to preserve democracy and the rule of law and instead prefer a radical free-market and devastating, authoritarian, counter-revolutionary violence—all while corruptibly preaching *freedom*. It brings to mind Samuel Johnson's bitter indictment: "How is it that the loudest yelps for *liberty* come from the drivers of Negroes?"

I've never been a conservative, in a fairer sense or with any mixture of right-wing demagoguery. It is well-noted, indeed obvious, that deregulatory capitalism, Friedmanism or Hayekian economies on crack, are antithetical to conservation, conservatism, and the preservation of culture, of local tradition, or nature. A less corporatist variety of conservatism, even anti-capitalist conservatism, may be less destructive but cannot protect life and does more to neuter and impoverish it. Parochial, inflexible defenders of culture do more, in bleak irony, to dull, stagnate, and kill custom and tradition. We can, however, navigate ideas and borrow their elements without subscribing to projects, or even to fundamental principles; much like a thief appropriating wealth for better use.

I don't expect much, but sometimes we need a basic reminding. We have many sentiments, often conflicting, with labels that are always inadequate, and we all dip into the pool of ideas robbing each other. In this way, we can regard certain virtues, practices, values, without the baggage and the burdens of impoverished dogmas. Most people don't know what they want and give themselves silly names. Ideologies claim virtues they never maintain, and the gulf between ideas and regimes remains unbridgeable.

It might seem peculiar that I'm having this struggle, yet there is a popular sentiment, a decent and compassionate sentiment, to preserve culture and architecture, art, objects, local spaces, living beings, that is definitely not reactionary and cruel or exclusionary. But mean and unsavoury sorts, and righteous ideologies, are so vocal, in a fetishistic way, about the preservation of things that one can mistakenly believe the wish to protect and conserve, and not so callously replace old things, is a nasty or even exclusively right-wing disposition. This mistake is understandable when so many rose-tinted and perverse nostalgists, ahistorical and false recoverers of history, proliferate in modern spaces—and modernity does little to be a good caretaker. Or when opponents of the right care less about antiques...

Modernity may often hurt us; we make this situation worse if we let others claim dominion over the past. We do ourselves a disservice if we let our opponents monopolise symbols, images, and ideas, let alone practical activities. If a misbehaving conservative says it is bad to neglect a Norman castle, that doesn't mean it is now good to do so. Heritage and history, very obviously, are not exclusively the domain of cultural conservatives—yet we can somehow forget this: we allow them to steal it. More progressive and fairer-minded people are mistaken, in wanting to improve our lot, if they do away with any old thing just because it is dated, pressing everonward with the newfangled and fashionable.

At the risk of snobbery, one can say that poverty and deprivation may impose a particular condition, a ruinous and impoverished state where one may not believe in much: judging how they are seen, noting the neglect of their welfare, the distressed state of their immediate environment, and the opacity of political institutions—one may ask: *Why should I care?* Why would one care for community and culture, let alone a few classical buildings, birds, and musty heritage sites when little care is afforded to you and immediate vices are easier? We can condemn this as callous, and poverty cannot be a blasé excuse for bad behaviour, but is it not understandable, and readily attested to, that a poor state of affairs may lead this way? And who is the author of this state of affairs? We ask a lot of people. Those who demand so much, in the realm of ideas, still maintain a world where waste and cheap clothes matter more than anything so sentimental and quaint as virtue or the conservation of trees.

I want to wear older clothes. Not out of a sense of nostalgic sentimentality, which still might creep in, but because it is better to maintain an old outfit than wear through new garments like meals. Clothing should not be so wasteful; so effluent. Society should not be, either. If we want to conserve the past, or physical representations of the past, then we need a more equal and judicious present.

The liking of history should not mean cultivating crude and cruel ideas. Such an attachment makes more sense as a reprieve, an escape, a guard against a world where so much may soon be lost in any number of ecological catastrophes or democratic upheavals, often with little hope. Nostalgia for what's lost forever need not be so obscene. In rare moments we can really feel the past, the stones do speak, and it need not always be so terrible.

Winter 2024

ON KNOWING THE PAST

OST fail at history. The past cannot truthfully, without prejudice or an idealising influence, be understood by modern people applying contemporary epistemology and all the subsequent amendments of technology and custom. This failure occurs among cultural *conservatives* and with those who are not so regressive. Conservatives fail as they wish to return to a fake, glorified, and distorted past that never existed and never resembled their moral inclinations. Our currently prolific ex-conservative authoritarian ideologues make the same mistake and make it worse. Progressives fail as they too cannot conceive of the past, the ways people lived, how they perceived the world, not coloured by modern influences. Modern influences, of moral character, language, psychol-

ogy, or epistemology, may derive from past philoso-
phies and politics, yet whatever ways we have of per-
ceiving the world today, the air we breathe, any latent assumptions on nature, life, or being, become
disconnected and removed — having evolved into a
new phenomenological species, with the past now
extinct. For everyone here, and for too many in-
between, the past is less something to be studied
and learnt from than something to be selectively
mined for acutely contemporary concerns, thus as-
suring current moral superiority.

Is the past, then, unrecognisable? No, hopefully
not, but I see no-one, or no more than a scant few,
who can imagine history and embody the minds of
our ancestors without deference to the epistemological traps of today. We are always stuck in our
time. Whatever morality I myself may agree with is
modern, my conception of politics and philosophy
is modern, and its past influences still result in a
view of life that is, through time and change, distant and even unrecognisable to the dead. I cannot
begin to ever thoroughly understand, say, medieval
life as I cannot truly escape today. This may seem banal, but it is worth remembering. We cannot render
the past with unimpeachable accuracy, overcoming

all our significant linguistic, cultural, political, and technological developments.

I see representations of the past that align with my moral and philosophical sensibilities, but they do not reflect accurate history. I do not think this history is impossible, with true feelings and ideas now beyond us, but it is at any rate more difficult to address.

Read many current accounts of history and it is easy to tell, from language, attitude, ideological maps, and any view on how life functions, that it was written in the 21st century by people tempered, or trapped, by present-day thoughts—to the extent that they are alien to their historical subjects. This does not mean we are necessarily morally wrong, nor does it mean we should replicate the morality of the past, but our ability to understand the biography of historical people is tremendously limited. Our world is that of now. The past is not just a foreign land: if we stretch the analogy and repeat ourselves, it is a different planet inhabited by extraterrestrials. Resemblances in behaviour are superficial—I do not trust us to be able to reveal or accurately portray a different scope of knowledge, a different phenomenology, a different way of conceiving everything. We have evolved, though that does not mean we have progressed—only that we have changed. Language, and the limits of language determining thought, particularly shows just how different thought once was and now is. It is not impossible, while maintaining ourselves, to render this different life, yet it is harder to see when obscured by our own prejudices—and across the entire political spectrum. We all fail. The map of history we have, what dates are noted, who we are occupied with, none of this depicts life and events from a true view of the dead; rather, it shows life through several filters of modernity—basically a caricature. We do not have to go back far to corroborate this. What did Samuel Johnson think? How did he think? How was he able, given his influences, to think? What capacity did he have for thought? From any angle most are confined and unable to think beyond their current mores — stuck within our current paradigm. We can answer about ourselves, not Johnson.

Life is seen as a timeline, a chronological order, with events and a teleology bending towards justice, progress, or some other ideal. Moral regression or political upheaval are seen as temporary setbacks or necessary backwards steps in order to take two steps forwards; often for a nebulous historical goal. A sense of historical progress feels almost intuitive, to the extent that it is insulting and frightening for many to suggest otherwise. What we want, what is best for us, or what is morally good is not practically, politically, mechanically, spiritually, or metaphysically inevitable. It is unsatisfying to think that on the level of events there is *no automatic selection which conforms with our moral requirements*—though that is probably the case.

To gain a glimpse of what life was like for people in another era we need to understand our own time, how it developed and came to be, and know how removed—or not—any historical subjects are from it. This does not excuse or justify the past, and rather is an attempt, as much as possible, at experiential accuracy. It is fine to condemn the past as a contrast to our current moral grounds, but we should first be accurate. That the past was often horrific is obvious, yet this fact is treated as if it were a rare novelty, with those who relish in declaring it so for their own ego. Nasty history does not mean we are morally improved, or that we will progress. Many do not understand the present by understanding the past and our chronology. Instead, the past is understood in reverse, fixed with present customs, with a forgotten or obscure development, where comprehensible yet dull ideas are employed to make easy, comforting analogies. Almost all historical analogies are inaccurate in some way. It is difficult to think like a medieval peasant. It is much easier to think of an observable, accessible modern image, deformed and twisted by time, as if left out in the weather and no longer recognisable, and think that was as it always was. I cannot suggest that someone from the past is really an alien, with a morality as well as a psychology that does not resemble contemporary humanity. Indeed, there are moral, ethical, and psychological resemblances that a 21st century person and a 13th century person share.

Instead, while we are alike, we underestimate how different we are — the past is transformed into a flat cartoon, holding our current thoughts while dressed in *cosplay*. We do not understand the past in forward gear, we learn it and comprehend it backwards, from the present, even if we do not wish to. Present ideas develop after a gestation, influenced by the past. But this development is hardly recognised. The current state of the world is as it is due to history, but few, myself included, understand this process. The historical narrative is constantly distorted by the end result; the long backwards shadow. A common phrase says that people are a product of their time. The overabundant equipment and overwhelming industry of modern life make this ever more so for us. The past as some pure form cannot exist. Cliché as it is, the past becomes an invention of the present rather than the present a product of the past.

�֍

Beyond real history, much historical fantasy and fiction face a similar impoverishment. Much *fantasy* is a Walt Disney act of historical fiction with old props on an old stage addressing contemporary sensibilities and conceived in a mind that can only recognise contemporary sensibilities (of whatever political, moral, or psychological persuasion). This is sometimes fine, yet it means modern fantasy moves beyond a purpose of older myth-making. It is familiar, agreeable, and far too obvious. Of course I may agree with and recognise an allegory for political autonomy and some other message I am happy with, yet dressed in Renaissance clothing. Nevertheless it is a modern story—a story that would be identical in a science-fiction future or in present-day Britain. It is the present day in fancy dress. I enjoy the clothing, the styling, the swords and the magic, but there is not much in the way of myth. We lose myth— which requires us, in part, to suspend understanding and tell a story regardless of our personal attachments. Sometimes I am eager for true escape, myths and allegories that may contain a moral lesson but are truly fantastical; psychologically, spiritually, existentially confusing; and not me. Not some easily accessible moral or message I agree with, but a creative story.

None of this is out of reach. For now, testimonies from the past still exist. History with more density, more depth, shared, and with more of an imagination about how our inner lives have changed is possible. The case for a more accurate picture of the past is banal but nonetheless true. Accurate history reveals social, maybe civilisational decay. Historians often play Cassandra, warning us of civil degeneration and the collapse, or at least the faltering and decline, of empires and kingdoms. We have a better description of our current malaise, institutional decline, a crisis of trust, and sociological devolution, if we can sense the echos of history. I'm not optimistic about what can be done, or prevented, but I'm not gloomy enough to give up. Much of the future will be like the past—similar tragedies, similar tyrannies, similar deaths. We cannot rely on our immediate environment alone. However uncomfortable it is, we deserve accuracy and something closer to the truth, as elusive as it may be.

Winter 2025

REMEMBERING GRACIÁN

HAVE been re-reading Baltasar Gracián. I was gifted a copy of *The Art of Worldly Wisdom* some years ago and picking it up again felt easy, as it is slim and digestible while still greatly stimulating. Few do so well in so slim a book, but the quality of words mean more than the quantity. Composed by the author as an oracular handbook, the reader feels free to open the text to any page to discover what awaits. As Gracián would agree, I read to work my mind—not my biceps with a heavy tome.

Gracián has always been acceptable to me, and an inspiration for others I'd also concur with. He distills the necessary contradictions of Montaigne into accessible affirmations rather than hiding his guidance in larger essays. Gracián's words are more difficult to take to heart, however, than philosophical or intellectual considerations I can easily store away and bring to hand when needed, as he often wonderfully expresses the best ways to behave, the best attitudes, ideas of graciousness and good judgement, the best ways to be prudent with our emotions and our impulses. He is the superego, suggesting how one should behave, although gratifying one's passions is easier. As such I often forget what Gracián says when it is most important in the heat of human interaction, and the wisdom is only recalled in hindsight. Memory is often unruly, or stupid.

Picking a favourite aphorism is difficult, but this one is particularly pertinent: "*Substance* is not enough, attention to *circumstance* is also required. A bad manner spoils everything — even reason and justice—a good one supplies everything, gilds, even sweetens truth, and adds a touch of beauty to old age itself. The *how* plays a large part in affairs, a good manner steals people's hearts. Fine behaviour is a joy in life, and a pleasant expression can help you out of a difficult situation in a remarkable way."

This seems eminently acceptable to me, even if I am personally poor at behaving well. It is a great example of an almost timeless cliché. It is good to be polite. It is good to know how to navigate a sit-

The Art of Worldly Wisdom

Baltasar Gracián

uation tactfully. Nonetheless some contemporary audiences will label this suggestion, especially in a volatile context, *tone-policing;* or insist it is an outdated form of 'respectability politics'. Sometimes malign groups will pick up and weaponise a good notion, which is often the excuse for abandoning good manners, given terrible people ask us to be polite, critique our methods, or demand we act with decorum. Yet we cannot allow them to rob us of good principles and good character. We may believe so much in the substance of a cause that any rude behaviour is tolerated. I object not to rudeness in itself so much as how ineffective it is and how self-righteous, and arrogant it is. One can be polite and arrogant too, but rude arrogance is the fad.

This results in moral activists (agreeable or not) who use such highly political language to become depoliticised. Real politics happens beyond and regardless of them while they performatively and expressively protest, rudely, or violently, or not—reduced to tedious slogans. They are not effective.

If impropriety works, then fine. But it often doesn't and many apparently cannot be convinced of this, as for them substance and personal grievances, however correct, because they are correct, seem to be enough. Tactics and tact are alien to them.

That these actions are resented is unsurprising. Without giving myself too much credit, I echoed a similar sentiment: "It is not so much about being correct, I could reasonably say that my political opponents are terrible people or at least have terrible ideas, but this is complaining — not effective change. We can forgive ourselves for outbursts against the most horrible of people, especially when they have harmed us, or traumatised us, and we're not expecting people to speak and act politely. If impropriety works on occasion, it is welcomed. The real contention, here, is efficacy."

The nature of resentment is always poorly considered. Terrifying people who resent the appearance of superiority are unfortunately a great political force today. Moral-political activists, however technically or academically correct they are, would do well to consider this. Resentment of their hubris and bad form is what they generate more than good change. It is not so simple to denounce that truth. No reasonable person doubts the weight of injustice. That injustice is very real means one needs to be effective rather than only expressive. I care little for expressive politics that shouts and screams a lot, and may shout and scream all while speaking the truth, but leads nowhere.

I have not mentioned the useless, actively counter-productive free marketing for one's opponents in being so susceptible and easily distracted by trolling and bait. This is worse than involving oneself in petty scandals that debase anyone who speaks of them. So many resources are wasted in the theatre of superficially political content, while the physical, actionable designs of one's opponents press along unhindered and actively encouraged by salacious attention.

I dislike chastising fellow victims, yet the success of noble causes is dear, and too much action for good has somehow neglected better presentation, and believes it be hollow or needless, or a tool of our opponents. Many truly believe the substance of their injustice is enough. Again, no reasonable person doubts this substance, but it is never enough. Worse, the manner in which many activists present themselves is arrogant, hubristic, wasteful, contemptuous, cruel, dismissive, divisive, rude, vulgar, and sows deep resentment—all because substance is considered enough. When they face a deeply resentful backlash, when their divisiveness begets even worse illiberal behaviour, they cannot conceive of even a small part of this as being their own doing.

We are all, in various ways, responsible for how our peers behave — also when they behave badly. We can admit responsibility for this without being guilty. When my fellow citizens do something horrible, I am in some part responsible for it. Or rather, as citizens we are responsible for each other, but not guilty. The idea of being guilty for how others behave, as being one's own terrible fault, is such a pernicious feeling that even the subtle responsibility anyone has for how their actions affect others is too close an association and too much to bear.

If one is a victim of great injustice, it is comforting to find agreement in a comprehensive idea or movement that has brilliant answers and an exacting path to follow. Many such movements do speak the truth, and surely do note very real terror, but not always and not absolutely. If more honestly diagnosing the wrongs of the world means being more uncomfortable, and not providing definite answers, it is then painful to begrudge our dishonesty.

This will be dismissed. Extreme and revolutionary politics, rejecting such a quaint artifice as good manners and good form, are much more aesthetically and emotionally appealing. And therefore more easily intellectually convincing, even if dishonest. Once one is seduced by such an encompassing epistemological and ideological map of how everything works, whether decently coherent or closer to an inarticulate set of vague but powerful commitments, the world and events are answered. They just have to fall in line with one's agreeable ideas. If they don't, it is not your fault. Others maliciously interfered.

It is better to resist all such parables and grand schemes, whether from the left, centre, right, western or eastern, but that requires prudence and discernment, and living with uncomfortable tensions; with a sense of the unknown and unpredictability, confusing and contradictory instead of cogent and familiar. I am not stuck here, though. I am content to abandon good graces and be vulgar when it works, and I am happy to consider the tactics of brute force and immodesty instead of moderation and diligence. Gracián, as ever, has the ability to contradict me: "Do not take payment in politeness; for it is a kind of fraud." Or further, ". . . avail yourself here of the nimbleness of good form, for the same truth that wheedles one, cudgels another."

There is a danger in being excessively lucid, in not being impatient enough, though there is no shortage of impatient and vulgar sorts saying what needs to be said in different ways. Being *reasonable* is never so interesting.

✳

Sometimes only brief words can produce superfluous thought. I'm sure Gracián was not considering the modern context of my intemperate peers, or my own folly.

I should not hold my views too firmly. "Every fool is fully convinced, and everyone fully persuaded is a fool." And more: in my above opinion, I am not the best at being courteous—surely, to some, I appear rude for suggesting so bluntly that many are vulgar or insulting.

The above, with all its pontificating, is speaking ill of people. I critique others harshly despite my own sensitivity and fear. "He who speaks ill will always hear worse." Something to worry about, but that worry will not always correct me. There is much to gain from Gracián, and a more concentrated effort in re-reading him may give me different insights each day.

Gracián's superego will have a hard time overcoming Goldsmith's id, which is sure to be forever ungracious. For all his talk of prudence and reserve I often do not follow, and I do not hold my tongue. Still, there is no-one, however wise, who does not regret his youth or his embarrassments, or finds his memory disagreeable and wishes to demolish it for something far better. Yet I should not resent myself. One can only become wise, in the ponderous way we acquire wisdom, by recognising our risible or loathsome personalities that come before our better selves.

Wisdom appears easy but is often demanding to truly accept. Let us hope for some consolation.

Winter 2025

ON ANNOYANCE

NNOYANCE is a milder emotion than bigotry, and we are often terribly annoyed by the manner and attitudes of friends and people we agree with. Annoyance often derives from a discomfort between an undesired voice, a presence or action, and an agreeable or desired environment—or perhaps better said: it is an unwanted distraction from conscious thought or a preferred atmosphere. I am most annoyed by my friends and family, not my enemies. I want to explore the manner in which I too am annoying, and why I, personally, am annoyed at so many things all the time. I will keep this grumpiness brief and not write anything substantial . . . to avoid annoyance.

Perhaps my curtness will be found annoying.

How I have written this article may be a source of annoyance to those who prefer certain styles, but let's put that aside for now. No matter what literary, journalistic, formal or informal style this is written in, it is bound to annoy *someone*.

I was vaguely annoyed when I learnt about the existence of formal, academic 'Annoyance' and 'Boredom' studies, declared professional disciplines. Given no prior knowledge, I thought immediately, with a knee-jerk prejudice, that this was some sort of over-scrupulous, positivist, scientistic systematising of a concept that is too diffuse and obscure to be confidently ordered; just as I might view psychology or economics. I was annoyed at the new knowledge, and then annoyed at myself for my dismissiveness.

What's particular, or peculiar, about my sense of annoyance is how curmudgeonly wide-ranging it is. It is not that I cultivate any particular hatred for most of what enters my realm to piss me off, as hatred would require more energy and might be construed as a compliment in reverse, but my austere disrespect for all ages and classes and faces can still be acute in each instance; where a lofty distaste for anti-intellectual delinquents rests in bed, in some freakish versatile coitus, with disdain for snobbish intellectuals.

Particular eccentricities are tedious. Eccentricities that appear as an organic part of one's person are tolerated, but these are hard to come by, like striving for authenticity if one is trying too hard. Odd things can be delightful, but many won't find them so. Oddities in fashion or manner are tolerable if one isn't trying; like *Sprezzatura*, the Italian art of effortless grace, which is to say, making the difficult easy. Otherwise, eccentricities in behaviour or presentation appear *affected.* Affectations are fine in jest but not as part of everyday character. Many possess affected manners, through insecurity, wanting to stand out or stand in, or to distinguish themselves in some way, though most such signs cause judgement or contempt. It is hard to suggest how to avoid this. Someone somewhere will always find any particular thought or action personally offensive due to their own idiosyncrasies, even if what they object to is good, but we can mostly forget people like that. The mild suggestion might be to try to be more comfortable in one's own skin, and as such find less reason to affect our style and conduct, though that is a lot to ask.

Depending on your mood, all of the above may be found annoying (as if I am anyone to suggest anything), and can be dismissed. Or aesthetics alone may be reason enough: as maybe my writing is *affected*, even if I'm mostly a sort of chameleon naturally adopting elements from what I've read. Regardless, that too can be uncomfortable. It still might seem like an imposition. Or I might easily be a bore.

Too often I find the over-committed, the over-certain, those too full of passionate intensity, to be the most annoying. They are particularly overzealous in their certainty despite the sparseness of their reading, or the surplus of time they have spent skulking around social media. Yet — with a rejoinder anyone observant enough might predict—those who seem the opposite of the former, which is to say, more aloof, too ambivalent, apathetic and careless, are similarly irritating. It is a commitment to superfluous intransigence, the hateful, closed and locked-down kind, that damages most. To be committed but open, with few truly settled convictions (especially in firmly academic philosophy), yet still having strong views . . . is not a contradiction. It is too easy to be committed but closed. Few approach this kind of moderation, I can hardly be said to do so, and it is annoying that we are so inept. A lesson I should probably learn is to accept, in some part, while remaining posed against our inherent human unreasonableness. This is far easier to accept as an abstract intellectual position than as an immediate feeling. There is a real danger in being too cautious, but I usually prefer it to being too bold—or arrogant . . . and therefore annoying.

The smartest or most accomplished can be terrible people, or at least too smug and overbearing, hence annoying. Lesser people, not as morally sound or brilliant, can make better friends and prove more reliable in both everyday or desperate situations. Some of the greatest minds in history have been annoying personalities. The polymath Gottfried Wilhelm Leibniz, for all his many accomplishments and creative excellence, was known to be confident to the point of great immodesty, socially awkward, boastful and exaggerative. Being skillful and technically gifted mean less to many if one is clumsy and patronising. The arrogant may protest, thinking the substance of their work is enough, yet neglecting tact, good taste and good form makes life difficult. Their superiority is detested even more so for being vulgar, and success would be more forthcoming if great yet vain and egotistical people were more discerning and socially aware—hence less annoying.

What I find most annoying about myself is my impulsiveness. I can rarely defer any need for quick satisfaction or comfort, though thankfully only with respect to minor vices. The major ones are too physically tiresome or distant; too annoying to even begin. I am sensitive to change and to sincerely rude behaviour, and I am emotionally fragile as well as physically frail. People comment on an apparent stoicism I display in the light of morbid subjects, but this front soon fails. I am quick to lose my cool and become temperamental, and I overshare. This is my natural disposition, and it is frustrating. Becoming a more prudent person able to better cope with the world's vices *and* my own is onerous.

Ideally, I should aim to find myself less annoying, if only for the sake of my own health, while annoyance at the outside world is not always so bad. It may be unhealthy, or hurtful, but a banal and obvious truth worth stating is that exasperation is a sure indication that something is wrong. It is hard to begrudge ourselves when we instinctually become animated and rude, even in an annoying way, or in an ineffective way, as the world, society, our institutions, give us sufficient cause to be distrustful or upset. The fact that the world is currently becoming less just, more unsafe, less trusting or trustworthy, is more than a source of annoyance. It is a reason for deep concern. Annoyance is doubled when we react incapably. Unfortunately the world and its denizens will only become more annoying in time, though this may give others an opportunity to be less annoying. Observe the most risible features of your country, class, age, nationality, etc, and work to avoid them. Their absence will merit you a hearty congratulation. Yet if too much effort is put into avoiding annoyances, the inevitable irony rises again.

Annoyance is inescapable. I used the words *annoying, annoyance,* or *annoy* at least 39 times in this essay. I fear repetition without good context is a common annoyance. And now, I find myself unable to end these thoughts in a non-annoying way.

Winter 2025

NECESSARILY HYPOCRITICAL
LUDDISM

ISTRUST of technology is difficult, and especially difficult to maintain as a public stance when we value the fruits of technology so highly. One who distrusts is quickly labelled as some sort of primitivist, conservative, intransigent Luddite incapable of accepting inevitable change, like an old man yelling at clouds, soon dead and irrelevant in the face of the massive power of new and hopeful technological opportunity.

A more discerning position against some but not all new technologies is portrayed as a shallow technophobia opposed to new and wonderful advances, rather than the elucidation of a banal but significant point: that some technologies are wonderful while others are potentially terrible.

I am not in a position to refuse technology in favour of a frugal life by Walden pond. I am ill and my survival depends on advances in science that have never before existed; and I live, thanks to medicine that has never before been possible, in the only time in history in which someone like me could possibly survive. Were I born in any other era before the 1990s I would have died at birth or as a young child. By which I mean that it is impossible for me to underestimate just how vital new technology is to my life. Dense, myopic technophobia is not my position.

The far more popular disposition today, well-articulated or not, is a science-fiction technological optimism, a pervasive scientistic faith (not a belief in the basic validity of science and the scientific method, but the sweeping application of a pseudoscientific understanding of science where it does not suit—judging value, morality, politics, economics, etc.), and the idea that technological advancement will eventually, almost naturally, mend our structural and social issues, coupled with amazing hype and the authoritarian tendencies of ultra-rich feudalists. This is a horizontal religion, often with indistinct tenets but still tremendously popular and just as lamentable as the vertical faiths promising their salvation. Their hubris is immense, and any tendencies towards messianism should be opposed. To argue against these answers makes one cynical, a pessimist, far too gloomy and popularly called a 'doomer', so the opponents of new technology are dismissed on appearances alone. I can renounce popular *doomerism*, while knowing that naive arrogance, sycophantic parables and inflated optimism are clearly not the only alternatives to morose death.

My aforementioned vulnerability, my special dependence and absolute reliance on particular technologies, means I fear what the world will become more than I believe any decent land will be left for us. Not all technological development is good. Many view 'technology' as a monolithic set of useful tools, an advance in aviation considered comparable to one in healthcare or in the media. But no, technology is ideological; its presence and its use shapes how we do things, how we conduct our lives, how we organise society and how we see life itself. Technological progress does not come immediately in hand with any moral progress either. The law and culture are always behind rapid industrial and technological development, meaning: we become disillusioned as much as others eagerly embrace the new toys. Industrial, technological societies, with the imperative of production, can never absolutely overcome the dissatisfaction they produce no matter how they are organised: whether according, superficially, to capitalist or communist rules. Industrial advance creates unrest, not just opportunity, and it is a common feeling that technological progress does not immediately produce a better economy and cultural prosperity. Instead, living standards regress as technology works in uncomfortable congress with questionable political and economic principles. Many technologies are brilliant and indispensable for a good life. Yet we have such a poorly conceived view of how we should live with ever-advancing technologies that are a series of Pandora's boxes.

Many advances in media technology (television, the internet, and now LLMs) have a few acute advantages and assets I cannot argue against, but after a rough tally of all the pros and cons, have a generally negative, corrosive effect on culture and organised society, atomising and divisive—at least if my bad-tempered estimation is worth anything. One of my most *conservative* beliefs, seemingly old-fashioned and square, is the need for a coherent social fabric, with civic and social institutions in good health,

general solidarity for all citizens and shared community. Rather than improve this, the most effective new social and informational technologies have
been predominantly disruptive, with progenitors actively commending and gloating at their disruptive
impact. They have contributed to social decay and
civic vandalism, great feelings of disinhibition, confusion, distrust, betrayal, unease, and the worsening
idea that what happens socially, politically, industri-
ally, is an opaque and undemocratic process where
the ordinary citizen is powerless, insignificant, unable to have a say, and unable to reckon how anything happens at all.

This outweighs, in quantity and quality, whatever virtues otherwise arise and what content I
might still find admirable.

Unhealthy reactions to this are unsurprising,
with people reacting to a bad situation by making
it worse. And so an increasingly detestable political
life is unsurprising. These feelings are compounded
by how speedily and without delay we continue
life. Never has slow and cautious reflection been so
unpopular. And so many flashy ways of distantly
speaking to each other, with what good they still
bring, with all the ways they confine and set the
boundaries of social organisation, may appear in-

ferior to now outmoded ways by which we could communicate or arrange our lives; at least for meaningful connections and learning, or a healthy community.

Here is a puerile complaint, or a romantic sentiment: old people are no longer *old*; no longer do they do what they were supposed to do. They don't quietly read the newspaper or stand as models of a bygone age. Now they are perpetual children, seated in front of the TV while playing games on their phones. Distracting them from these habits causes a belligerent reaction that used to be stereotypically teenage but has now become a custom of our elders. *Real* old people are dying out, their once youthful replacements no longer age gracefully but maintain the vices of adolescence. I remember when screens were supposed to give you 'square eyes' . . . What difference is there now between the child spending most of the day strained over an iPad and the retiree ineptly slapping an over-tuned Samsung while simultaneously peeking at the TV, making daft Facebook comments on fake pictures? Ageing is yesterday's fad; who needs it? It is too easy to make a patronising comic: "Phone bad." Well, yes. Do we really want the old to die?

For all my complaining, I'm flippant; too general, too exaggerated. I'm no Jonathan Haidt—sweeping, simple and absolute. It is easy enough to find exceptions to all the worries about excessive technology. I'm not going to romanticise the old days. Common laments against an impoverished present are founded in cruel temptations, false history, and offer a worse or impossible alternative. Yet it is not as if these objections have no basis, even if too many are crude.

Artificial intelligence is terrible. Its dangerous ecological impact is clear, yet I'm more aware of its consequences for learning. Imagine being able to skip the process of learning how to write, learning how to acquire knowledge, learning how to read, learning how to order your thoughts and make good judgment, relieving yourself of such burdens with the help of a machine you do not understand. This sounds alarming, but that is what so many students now do. They vacate the process of learning, seen as a dull time sink and without value, as if the end product is all that matters. Professors without the time or energy to examine so many texts for sterile artificial involvement produce gormless students illicitly acquiring degrees with no understanding of how they got there—an upgraded version of paying for someone else to cheat your classes for you, and a mode that's somehow prescribed and supported by our largest and most powerful corporate and government entities. Forget actually reading Freud or Nietzsche, forget real knowledge, forget learning anything, slip it into the software and skip to the next question. Cheating was always possible—now it is incentivised, readily available, and easier than ever.

Universities do not have the time or resources to regulate the growth of AI, and ideas of academically embracing it are quaint and idealistic — we will see instead far more bad news than any novel highlights. Professors can mark AI papers just as they would conventional ones, and for now students shall deservedly receive bad or mediocre grades for being derivative and bullshitting. When LLMs can produce papers on Goethe and La Rochefoucauld that make a passing grade and can go undetected by overworked professors, we shall have all the problems described above. Students pass, but with no real knowledge of any subject, and this is the death of learning. They'll simply cheat en masse and not care, even delighting in not having to read. And universities, counter-majoritarian institutions in an insidious identity crisis since the 1960s, closer to commercial entities than places of learning or real qualification for work, attacked from outside and committing self-harm daily, won't mitigate these worries any time soon.

The original Luddites, worried about new automated machinery and woollen mills, have a poor reputation as their name is used as a byword for the narrow-minded fear of technology and change. Yet the Luddites were not morally inferior dolts. Automation upended and destroyed their way of making a living and their way of life, and it is hardly an unfamiliar or unreasonable sentiment to be worried about automation, monopolisation or other practices that leave one without work and damage a culture. The apparent inexorable and fashionable changes via technology are never a monolith, and enough myth and fable, or a basic knowledge of history, can show us the grim cost of our vanity and conceit in allowing them to alter our world unregulated and without care. Doing away with older technology and ways of life so expediently, or callously, notwithstanding all the very bad old ways of life that exist, means when one door opens, another closes. Our new infrastructure is fragile and still regularly susceptible to the elements, ecological disaster, political repression, or economic disorder. A basic power cut throws us into turmoil. Doing away with ways of life and work that should instead become dormant redundancies, fallbacks in case of emergency, neglecting plan B, discarding old forms in favour of new upgrades, means we are lost when the new system inevitably falters—having forgotten how to walk after learning how to run. Technology should be a useful enhancement, an option, not an obligation, and not given our total dependence while controlled by overpaid, egomaniacal oligarchs divorced from everyday life.

Technology may *progress*, but which sort of technology profits most is motivated by pernicious incentives, where this process, no matter the awesome innovations, occurs with historical regression or with us having to endure a world once enthused with a technocratic confidence now reaping part of what it has sowed. Enough has been written about the intellectually adverse results of information technology. I am thinking of Carl Sagan, Neil Postman and numerous others. My own contribution means little. The awful politics, authoritarian deceits and current democratic decay are not a new future aberration but maybe something more in line with our longer and general history. The world post-1989 may be considered a height of democratic prosperity; a truth that might appear deeply pessimistic.

The near future will be worse for the health of our societies, and some fantasise about the magic of technology to end this horror, to bypass muddy human affairs and reach a utopian peak beyond the petty scandals of our politics—as if life under the machine or directed by impersonal algorithms will be glorious and without issue.

> History is dramatic. If the time should ever come when a few men were, or believed themselves to be, 'masters and possessors over social nature', then perhaps the drama would be over. But the individual would have forfeited his sense of liberty. Would a life subjected to a rational or purposeless organisation still be human?
>
> —Raymond Aron, *Progress and Disillusion: The Dialectics of Modern Society*

Gaudy technological optimism, and the rambling pseudo-philosophies of rich technophiles, are part of an ideological model, a paradigm, an unsophisticated but persuasive unworldly rearrangement of life, and its prophets should be doubted. If one promises deliverance and salvation, or damnation and catastrophe, it is better to doubt. I don't care for fantastical visions or quixotic schemes. Avoiding the worst outcome means more than achieving the best, and the prevention of tragedy is worth more than dreams.

Instead of finding solutions, the technological utopians, or at least the cynical providers of our digital world, have been instigators of our current malaise. Their lack of regulation and care as they speed ahead of culture, human agency and the reach of legal systems, causes more harm than what novelty their platforms may bring. Maybe I am too harsh, but the conduct of social media companies is hard to defend. There is certainly pressure from the superego to accept the supposed advancement of civilisation; yet what is deemed best for all is inevitably used as a weapon against us.

Auguste Comte's positivist utopian project was arguably benevolent yet doomed to fail. Contemporary society still enjoys the flavour of wishful scientism and all-encompassing *theories of conduct* despite history or reason. Others suggest utopian projects are superficially alluring but inevitably harbour nightmares, and their failure is welcomed, as we should be careful what we wish for . . . Past utopians were 19th-century socialists or rural religious sects who were all rendered impotent by reality. The *utopians* we should fear today are not futile online conspiracy theorists, useless leftist cranks, or philosophical naval-gazers eager for fantasy, but authoritarian billionaire technophiles (with demagogic right-wing appetites) who have *actual* influence and power. Their zealous dispositions and puerile commitments will plausibly flatline just like their historical utopian predecessors. Sometimes it is better for all of us that ambitious men fail rather than succeed.

We lose something with every apparent leap forward, and to say so is not mere traditionalism. The ideal future cannot reach its peak by forgetting the past. Civilisation can only advance sustainably, morally and socially, with a measure of prudence and without forgetfulness. And who among our current rulers, or saleable pundits, shows any prudence or fit memory?

Regulation of the internet is inept or inevitably oversteps. My protests are intolerant. I have no clear answer how to manage our overwhelming mess. We cannot return to an idealised past, false and misleading, and the nostalgic will to do so will be unproductive. It is not a sound political strategy to wait for the world to return to how it was. *"Normal"* won't return. Our future will not be sublime, and I struggle to hit a hopeful note. If you can forgive me descending into platitudes, the worst people thrive on our hopelessness, and hopelessness is not a good recommendation for our health or polity. Historically we have managed to suffer desperate circumstances with radical hope and perseverance. It might be an impossible request to concentrate on better technologies and neglect the unfavourable ones, but that is about all I might childishly claim. Optimism may be possible, even if it now feels incoherent.

Spring 2025

BOOKSHELF BE JUDGED

E look at a friend's bookshelf and spot a work from a *problematic* author. The innards of the book or the reputation of the author are the basis of judgement. Somehow, the book's presence on the shelf says something about its owner—they surely like that book, enough to keep it, and have its spine on show to note their appreciation. Further, surely, the owner must accept as part of the bargain, the life of the author and the content of the work? The book is not only the owner's possession, it *is* the owner, identity manifest, and now judged.

This assessment happens in seconds. The mere presence of certain books is a 'red flag'. My above description is uncharitable; it may look crude and shallow, but such judgments are not uncommon. We soon know, within a breath, that the banal act of owning a book and displaying it on your shelf does not immediately convey love and agreement with the content or its author. We can appreciate things we dislike. We might value books as physical entities and records of life regardless of their subject. We can learn from opponents or villains. You can want a larger library, and without loving everything on your bookshelves.

A rushed appraisal of what particular books mean to who owns them is still not totally stupid.

Surveying my bookshelves, a young interest in Albert Camus is visible; one finds an interest in Montaigne, then secondarily in Tony Judt, and then an interest in Raymond Aron, Manès Sperber, Arthur Koestler, Leszek Kołakowski, Clive James, all linked, by what they all found worthy. Sections of my shelves reflect early interests organically expanded over time. A path can be traced. It appears very male at first, until one happens on Simone Weil, Susan Sontag, Martha Gellhorn, Toni Morrison, Svetlana Alexievich... Many of the books I own owe their presence in my room to a stream of intermediary interests. One becomes two and then four and so on, where who I appreciate recommends another. I try mostly to buy books I think will be good, based on my prejudices, so we cannot discount judging me by my library.

Still, others on my shelf do not owe their existence to being colleagues, friends, or fancies of their neighbours. The interests of any of them may be wide enough to stimulate random purchases, with flights from familiar territory to foreign realms on a whim. A flashy cover can be alluring enough to dispel a previous indifference, and I will read what is unusual for me. Not all the library is interconnected. Much on my shelves represents my interests and my studies, yet here too we still make an intellectual and emotional leap, rudely suggesting that anything on my shelf (and the authors I collect or feel most attuned to), must all, in supreme totality, be agreeable to me. If I have studied Camus and Aron so much, then surely that signifies that all their content is acceptable to me, you may ask. Does that mean that one's allegiances must become one's identity, one's passing interests must *be* you, and if someone were to disagree with Aron that I must feel personally insulted . . . ?

No, of course not. My sociological studies, philosophical curiosities or any views and dispositions do not equal my identity. If I admire someone it may mean I share their concerns or their methods, but not their views or personality. It seems ridiculous to draw this out and point out the trite idea that one cannot agree with every book one owns. Then why is this judgment so common? You can doubt me, but this notion of ownership and agreement is very real and not difficult to find among vaguely bookish people, or anyone else. When total agreement is not presupposed, one may still reason that any book on display must signal an acute allegiance. A political view is not a core commitment, though it is commonly assumed to be. A moral commitment should not be equated with one's core identity; a moral change does not have to alter one's root identity, yet it is still assumed. Identity consists of far more than moral and political positions, or a taste for certain genres. Political disagreement is considered an attack on one's identity, which is not always true though it is hard to convince many otherwise, especially with wider, venomous polarisation, and the adoption of a politics of enemies. Holding correct political beliefs doesn't immediately make someone a good person. I should add to this another obvious point: we need not find agreement with those, in politics, who want us dead. This still doesn't mean that a political idea, or a policy, should be a vital element in one's identity. An idea, a moral stance, a belief, or a book, doesn't capture identity.

Why does this line of thinking, the assumption of identity based on bookshelves and single ideas, happen? Even if one doesn't judge a person by the content of their bookshelves, they most probably make comparable rapid judgments in other spheres. It is easy, which makes it attractive, yet it is also algorithmic. Many of us want a fast assessment and valuation of a person. Our time is short and for survival's sake, or ease of living, a single instance must be extrapolated. In reality we can be complex sorts with numerous different answers to anything and everything, yet litigating every question in life is long and bothersome. Instead, if one flies a flag, or suggests a policy, or takes one particular moral position on a single issue, we can assume ten other positions and determine someone's life. We can condemn someone's entire person with the intel of a single comment. A flag can represent one-hundred different ideas, a net so broad that we can spend hours detailing reasons why anyone would parade a flag, either benevolent, malicious, or impartial. Prudence would say to reserve judgement and first gather more information, but it is less tedious to accept a common idea, or a predictable loyalty with all it would theoretically and practically entail, and move on.

A first intuition can be correct, regardless, but it is possible that we overextend our intuitive judgements. Experts, not just us laymen, are susceptible to algorithmic shortcuts: one's views and priorities slowly and imperceptibly change, still sincere yet inaccurate, through algorithmic incentives. Otherwise gifted voices can still accept an easy answer, whether because it is faster or because a difficult, equivocal analysis is less satisfying. Sometimes the vices we are open to, whether we know a lot or know very little, are matters of character more than intellect.

It is not just an issue in another's judgement. Rather than tirelessly working through every point or order, I offload the work to others — to those on my shelf. I defer to their expertise and authority, so it is not always silly or reductive to believe I align with everything Bernard Williams says. This is understandable, I know my limits, it is not only easier for others but easier for me to say I agree with someone and get on with my life. On closer examination I will clearly diverge, but who has the time to figure it out? I'm too impatient, and so are you.

We can escape these difficulties and be more astute in our estimation of others, yet this is harder than ever in a hurried, uncertain world. While we are at once exposed to a vast technological potential, the landscape of human interaction and ontology is also diminished. Our sociological backdrop, distrustful and uneasy, more often does not facilitate a deeper and more discerning consideration of theory and action. We are told, intimated, or motivated by the mechanisms of contemporary life, to be rash, bold, and impatient in advance of being lucid or subtle. Careless judgment is efficient with our current concerns. Not being anxiously judgmental is old-fashioned. Today, a person is deemed odd for not making an immediate comment (with no time to reflect), and *excessive lucidity* concerning human identity and interrelations is untimely and uncomfortable.

With so much going on in the wider world, the intemperate review of a bad book on a bookshelf is less surprising. If you do not judge a bad book on your friend's shelf harshly, then well done: more than others you remember not just the basics of a well-stocked library, but the depths of our relationship to knowledge; to one's tastes. It can make sense to judge someone for a bad book, and a sizeable collection of disagreeable books might say something about a person's integrity, but I'd rather wait before uttering too damning a pronouncement. It is vanity to only engage with subjects that align pristinely with one's own sensibilities. If I only kept books that I absolutely concurred with and found truly faultless, I might have only five or six. I might have none at all if I'm more thorough. Even more so, as a fickle author, I'd have to forsake my own.

Spring 2025

Principles and Possibility

HAT is possible? Many plans and schemes for human development, just or cruel, have made classic appeals to nature. Crudely we can say that everything is natural, or nothing is unnatural, and any of our designs or customs are not unearthly impositions from an alien asserting something impossible. All that's great or terrible may come from natural origins, if we are not unnatural outsiders, yet any basic overcoming of this classic fallacy can illuminate, instead, another distinction. Natural phenomena, such as the rudiments of biological processes or the movements of geology, are morally neutral, but their effects justly receive moral surveillance. Seemingly unnatural designs or creations of humanity rationality—assembled by our hand where they otherwise might not occur without our intervention and ingenuity, can be good or bad. Air conditioning and bicycles don't come into being without our intervention. Yet after this philosophically primitive exercise, familiar to anyone who's studied ideas professionally or not, most of us unprofessionally will still have a question not just about what is natural, but what is possible and what makes sense as an acceptable ontology.

Beyond inventions and gadgets, this applies to ideas and the organisation of civilisation. The most common appeals to what is a good or workable ideological organisation, or coherent political framework, claim with variable articulateness a natural or organic base. *The state of nature* is assumed to be a Rousseauian nobility or brutish hardship—with well-thought or ill-formed judgement of what is good or bad either way. I concur with a degree of *realism* (not the realism of international relations) one derives from Thucydides, Hobbes, or Machiavelli about the realistic limits of human vices and action — a *realism* that denotes us as self-interested and, without careful mediation, readily capable of great cruelty. As such, for a good life to have a chance it needs a degree of social or institutional deliberation. We lack the strength to follow reason fully, as per La

Rochefoucauld, or we accept Aron's "permanence of humanity's imperfection."

Poor readers of Hobbes imply that he somehow delighted in the brutish and short life, but he did not. Hobbes lamented our short lives and believed in a proto-liberal goodness we take for granted today. His method for achieving a better life, the supervision of the absolute sovereign, his reservations about democracy, are what we can question; yet the idea that Hobbes loved *Hobbesian* nature, poor and nasty, is untrue. He is not the first to be greatly misunderstood. Still, whether socialist, liberal, or conservative one can access human possibility, human capability, with this expectation— and the answers about how to organise our lives after these principles are diverse.

A great mistake is to think that cruelty or unjust systems of government, because they seem to appear *natural*, are good. A supposed natural origin is not a moral defence. I don't think a market economy, capitalism—or if we consider *neoliberalism* less an analytical approach than an inarticulate set of strong commitments, a false, magical primacy given to market (something done by apparent opponents of capitalism too)—is very good. The injustice of this organisation, becoming more unequal, feudalistic and authoritarian instead of competitive and democratic, is brutal. Defenders may say the brutality is natural and therefore good. I don't consider it *natural* in the same crude way, while I do believe it is unjust and preferably alleviated by our involvement in some way. If capitalism is not as natural as the development of eggs into foetuses, a differentiation that is probably true, I can say something else about it . . . Some ideas about the organisation of life are less organic. There are ideas opposed to capitalism that are arguably superior and better for the preservation of a fair society, but they are harder to implement or less aligned with popular human temperament. We instead are left with the question of whether an idea, imperfectly transforming into a practice, has an easier time coming into being due to its complexity or its level of rationalisation. An idea, a political plan, virtuous or not, can achieve a closer or more distant adherence to human vices or whatever we find easier to do. Societies have existed that have been distantly inhuman or exploited the monstrous capacity of the darkest reaches of humanity, with spoiled noble goals, intent ruinous zeal, or savage violence aiming to overcome a previous order or straighten the crooked timber of humanity. A society that strives to straighten and fix the human drama, as bad as our usual proclivities are, appears to have a harder time persisting than a plan (or action lacking a plan), unjust or not, that tolerates or unfairly delights in the easier path of self-interest and misery. An idea or a regime can undergo a more organic, habitual development, or it can be more of a rationalised imposition; trying to enforce an intellectual vision upon an impulsive populace. An imposition, less likely to become a sustainable form of government, can be morally justified or attain keen insights into human circumstance. It can be derived from works of genius, but that does not preclude its successful application to reality. Impositions upon reality may be religious, mystical, political, ideological or scientistic. The central planners were likely at fault for trying to pseudo-scientifically control the economy. They tried to impose politicised economics onto reality. Ironically, as it seems many haven't read their Hayek, modern deregulatory economics commits the same sin of scientistic positivism, trying to force a discipline to be *objective* (which relieves it of responsibility), and failing in a similar way to reckon with so many events and tendencies that go beyond such rational organisation. Economics, like politics and sociology, is not physics. The credibility of science is not at question. Indeed, we are questioning its ideological mis-appropriation in attempting to order our lives. We will always struggle to contend with how applicable our heavy interventions are to the human spectacle. From any derivation we may have to accept that many find themselves unfit.

❋

But what are we to make of the survival of our current situation? We live in a mixture of complex theory and, more often, makeshift implementations and unthoughtful habits. Most ideas are a mess of images that are convinced of their own coherence. The extent to which ideas align with more organic human predilections is debatable, yet I can assert an uncomfortable view, and one I risk repeating to the point of tedium: our moral requirements do not assume such an *automatic selection*. There is no rule in the process of history that makes it reflexively conform with better ways of life. The vices that underpin certain systems are easier. Capitalism exceeds economy. It is more than the administration of money. Articulated and well-argued defences of the market exist, though they persist more not due to much firm and analytical rigour. The impulses that underpin market structure are more closely aligned with classic *self-interest*. More, industrial progress results in similar disillusions no matter the arrangement: as capitalist technocracy or socialist technocracy; and all industrial and post-industrial societies are more similar to each other than to distant pre-industrial societies. The task of transcending alienation and anomy, a worthy endeavour, is not as simple as economic redistribution — though we can still argue for it anyway. Radical notions to outdo and overthrow the order, worsening at it is, become idealistic or given to magical thinking and desperate pleading. It is enough to say that many concerns about our lot, justified or otherwise, are not so stable and absolute. It is not that all such opposition is wrong. Some opposition is intensely articulate about our rot and rightly wishes to mitigate it, while other theories propose an even worse alternative. It is not the case that our current societal and economic organisation will last forever—it will one day fail and transform into something else. But not any time soon or so indisputably. Nor does the decline of the United States, accelerated by authoritarian trends, mean the wider collapse of a much

broader economic epistemology even after yet another market crash, dramatic inflation or massive
recession. With technophilic autocrats illicitly having their way at our disadvantage, such excesses and
the disparity in wealth will be intensified. The likes
of Russia etc., with their own debasement, engage
in a hyper-neoliberal might-is-right neurosis, coupled with fetishistic, destructive, quasi-mystically
inspired aims of global disruption, and desperation
to violently flex a fascistic imperial mania. Nor does
China forsake capital; it is imprisoned by the same
economic motivations and does not, somehow, no
matter what desperate ideologues say, propose an
opposite model outside global capitalism (or economic neo-feudalism, or whatever term one prefers).
It remains eagerly in this domain. It is democracy
that is unfortunately declining, while a worse variety of capitalism can still thrive at its expense, with
or without it. Some herald the collapse as a dream
come true, though mostly with demagogic tones. Instead, revolutionary notions often work with a different judgement of human possibility that for all
the honourable impatience with injustice can still
fail to grasp a measure of this realism; and that's before we contest the projects that are given to unbe-
lievable harm and cruelty.

It is worth repeating something I've written before: "What's still eternally of concern is what John Milton called 'the known rules of ancient liberty.' " This does not mean we are resigned to a slow and hollow Burkeanism. The socialist Proudhon, the liberal Tocqueville, and Karl Marx were all severe in their criticisms of the *imitators* of the Great Revolution, 'the comedians of 1848'. Mary Wollstonecraft, whose ideas we take for granted, knew the dangers of revolt much like others. The fight for liberty doesn't presume morality or good politics. To use another famous expression, it is one of the easiest and most regrettable processes for revolt and revolution, in the name of good causes or not, to be hoisted by its own petard. Pessimism becomes more reasonable, while we are hopefully not resigned to it. Strategy and good tactics are alien concepts to many revolutionaries. What miraculous formula is there that could rid us of our inequalities? This isn't some cheap question. It is easy for some to honestly answer, but this doesn't suppose intelligible, let alone politicised, ways of achieving it. I'm sorry for being doubtful; I'd much rather have fewer doubts and it is still much worth it, after all this caution, for people to optimistically dream."

A cautious and more doubtful assessment of human interest needs a level of lucidity, even if there is a danger that excessive lucidity may leave us stuck with a contemptible lack of confidence or action. It is fine to be impatient with our inability and to wish for more.

If we can accept our permanent imperfection, there are still methods of hopefully making use of our inclinations in a more suitable or judicious way. I vaguely attach myself to a liberal tradition (of Montesquieu, Raymond Aron, Isaiah Berlin, et al), and claim the *magical primacy* given to the economic market is a perversion of particular commitments. We have a thin, impoverished landscape of ideas today where opponents of neoliberal hubris, correctly defining its injustices, have a reduced scope of what ideas and people exist—naming things ineptly within a narrow frame. Too many of us, of any allegiance, have a shrunken idea of what ideas are possible and fail to expand discourse. We can accept that a technocratic centrism, with its particular bureaucracies and false, inflated assumption of its own inevitability risks failure. Hyper-identity politics begets more terrifying, contrary and resentful identity politics in the direction of our populist antagonists. Lack of intellectual humility and the appearance of aloof superiority only contribute to degeneration. Authoritarianism and the death of trust is our near-future. Sadistic, anti-democratic illiberalism is born of our failure. The current popular right wingers, the increasing number of extant administrations are a demagogic variety of post-conservativism—however well-realised that may be or not. One of their primary aims is not to preserve traditions but to break them; to break with previous political norms and social mores, via duplicitous language promising freedom while delivering the opposite: anti-constitutional, anti-democratic, undiplomatic, censorious, openly spiteful and vindictive stances. We must maintain the effort to preserve our institutions from the arson of deceitful despots and autocrats, and doing so means coming to terms not just with their noxious schemes but with our own deficiencies and the roots of our disenchantment.

There is a rich tradition in political thought that I don't exactly align with that still wishes for something better. I encourage explorations of these intellectual traditions. Even food I dislike has tasteful ingredients. This exploration is needed as it is the authoritarian populists who have managed to conjure an actionable vision of the future, frighteningly convincing to many despite its rank flaws, where the centre is diminished and the left is absent.

We can offer ideas, paths for future success that feel legitimate and meaningful, but doing so means having to contend with our failures yesterday and finding practical politics, not depoliticised political talk. Maybe a great change is coming, that is, should we remain optimists. Maybe the vices of men can be made to contribute to the good of the state, that is, should we remain pessimists. Both can still work together.

Hopefully, for the sake of our health, they will.

Spring 2025

University Decline

HERE are differences and shifting distinctions between professionalised theories in the academy and the methods of public intellectuals, and these are depreciated further by *pundits* and *commentators*. The boundaries can be strictly enforced, and each medium risks mockery for impersonal, elite and out-of-touch rumination—or for the effusions of squalid, shallow, easy-answer talking heads. The scorn comes from all directions, from above and below, and a fine recipe involving skilled professorship and journalistic openness is a rarer thing now than in past ages of letters. Technology has not aided intellectual pluralism; it has entrenched moods and sharply-delineated methods. Alasdair MacIntyre said some time ago that professionalising philosophy did more

to neuter its effects than religious or political repression. Public appetites can be crude, with ex-
ploitable desires for quick and uncomplicated solutions. Higher-minded sorts rightly don't wish to
sacrifice the integrity of their scholarship to appeal
to the lowest denominator. It is difficult to claim
the path of development for information and media
technology hasn't contributed to shaping a world
with these low hopes. Bare literacy is accepted, but
cultivated learning is more demanding. Regardless,
the idea of a most highly-cultured population faces
a demographic issue.

It should be less controversial to say that too
many students are expected to go to university. This
is controversial when right-leaning governments
wish for cuts to the academy and a diminishment of
its responsibility for unfair reasons: denigrating culture and attempting to reduce the necessary counter-
majoritarian role of the university. Many students
are pursuing degrees for non-existent jobs or have
degrees which don't suit the job market. Employers have fancifully decided that high-level degrees
are required for entry jobseekers. The health of the
university after events such as May 1968 is still
in question. Much of the crisis of identity born
then still lingers at the base foundation of a frag-

ile institution—we reject the idea of university as a solely technocratic tool or as one acquiescing to "the adaptation of education to possible careers." Traditionalist defenders of the university say "culture is an end in itself, above, beyond and incidental to any profession." Revolutionaries accuse technocratic recovery as acting "to save the bourgeois capitalist society, although socialist technocrats act in the same way." Others, fond of increased democratisation, say that adapting university to available professions "pushes students from lower classes towards inferior jobs." These are not invalid concerns. Though all these ideas, general culture, idealised revolution, and further democratisation still together prolong and aggravate the crisis of fewer appropriate careers and societal unease (quotations from *The Elusive Revolution: Anatomy of a Student Revolt* by Raymond Aron).

Despite the many initiatives forwarded by government or employers, we still undervalue and undernourish efforts towards vocational education as well as work that is inadequately paid. Ask around and you will see that most support the truth that many undervalued occupations are vital, yet this does not extend to giving them prestige or their fair renumeration. Much work is socially enfeebled and made a subject of snobbery. It is true that millions work in jobs with no motive for living. It is unfortunate that so many polytechnic universities were renamed in veiled disgust and turned into lesser versions of the rest.

But what is the university for? Why do we suppose millions of students should, as a preeminent and reputable goal, spend excesses on tuition? It is very difficult to convince the British public, or the public of any post-industrial society, that less-academically qualified work is not beneath them, and that one should pay healthily for such work, yet it also seems a reasonable suggestion, fitting the temperament of British students, to invest in and expand highly-skilled and reasonably paid vocational work rather than have so many attending academic courses that do them little good, or otherwise prolong a situation in which many students are proto-students studying almost any subject as a vague stepping-stone towards any sort of career, be it history, philosophy or whatever—it often matters little to them which—while the courses maintain little relevance to what they might do afterwards. It might be worthwhile for businesses to "suck it up" and not feel embarrassed to offer job opportunities where one doesn't need inflated degrees, although cynically one could say the universities are in a money-making business and this situation suits them too much to change—a terrible feedback loop where commerce and academia exhaust everyone, with neither achieving their respective ideal purpose. University is not a *preparation* if what it prepares you for is irrelevant to work yet required nonetheless, or if professions hold inappropriate ideas about the role of universities. I have reservations about my estimation of the university as I wish to see it prosper and be available for anyone capable, yet in the current situation we demand too much of the university. Moreover, its association with the workplace is malformed. We demand too much of students, demeaning their lives if they fail to attain the expected honours. It does not provide the greatest pluralism of opportunity for the best or only path to well-remunerated work to be through university. Rather than uplift the lower classes, these are forced into a confined, narrow route. This is unfair to experience and talent outside the academic mode. It is an old-fashioned and elitist idea that university should be for a minority, though hopefully a more diverse and equitable minority than before. Academia now exists as a preeminent milestone students are instructed to aspire to even when occupations and wider society should hold different expectations. There is another idea that is controversial in considering the acclaim for academia: a greater number of students attending university has not improved the quality of scholarship; nor does attending university mean that many students truly become scholastically more adept or knowledgeable. Farewell to the romantic image of an elite bastion of knowledge occupied by the most erudite and learned. It is easier than ever for students who don't care a jot about *real scholarship* or learning to sail through university, enrolling in courses seen as a cynical means to an end, and achieve qualifications. Consider the changes in education that started around the period of the Enlightenment. These are followed by a huge shift away from classicism towards the turn of the 20th century, the diffusion of truths per state in the 1950s, and finally the impact of the explosion of the internet and AI . . . this does not bode well for the longevity of the term *higher knowledge.*

> If the University is not a preparation for anything, it must be reserved for a minority; if it is to be open to a larger number, it must prepare them for more than reading Vergil with the aid of a dictionary.
>
> —Raymond Aron, *The Elusive Revolution: Anatomy of a Student Revolt*

The present problem, or a problem persisting from preceding decades, is: if students feel they must go to university to earn some valuable degree (in whatever field) or as the most fortuitous way to better their lives, there is still a great need for work we undervalue, that higher educated students consider below their station and deem fit only for the unfairly disregarded poor and exploited migrant labour. Nor has the university ever recovered from its old injuries. It still acts competitively to an extent that is traumatising. It is not properly adapted to professions nor are professions, now, adapted well to the ideal purpose of the university. Consumption and production can't give meaning to existence. A noble ideal might make the problem obsolete (such as Oscar Wilde's vision for the soul of man), but in the near term, we have little coherent idea of how to balance our imperfect contributions.

The more a society matures through the service economy and the more values progress, with the advance of technology and culture, the more its citizens reject an industrial hierarchy that won't disappear anytime soon. The perceived lower rungs of the societal ladder are no longer regarded as worthy for a greater number of us, which might be a fair assessment given inadequate conditions; but who is to do all that very necessary work more and more of us consider unbecoming of our talents? It is not so much the university itself that is causing social unease, but the expected aspiration towards university instilled from school and competitively imbued is still troubling. The esteem it is rewarded, with few viable alternatives valued so highly, with fewer adequate jobs existing without prior university experience, continues to nurture resentment. The health of the university and the economic health of the median person are constitutively tied to the fitness of democracy. Respect for *lower professions* (as well as their pay) needs to improve if we care not just about the honourable goals of human progress, but the raw survivability and sustainability of prosperous nations. Increasing inequality is no good for the health of supposedly *developed* nations. Neglecting this issue will result in greater disaffection and contribute more to democratic decline; and democratic incapacity means general political weakness and strategic inability. Whether you are Milton Friedman or Karl Polanyi, you are broken with the failure of democracy. The Americans or Europeans, leaning towards authoritarianism as a means of maintaining strength, instead commit self-harm and perpetuate their own economic and social decay.

If we are fine with outsourced migrant labour to carry out less desirable jobs, we still have the problem of the mistreatment of migrants and the common wish to lower migration. My personal admiration for other cultures is less noteworthy. The fact is, a wider population shows a far different (and negative) estimation, exploited by dishonest political actors whose only answer is demagoguery rather than anything real. My (perceptibly fairer or progressive) ideas are less popular or convincing. Immigration is not a process without issues, nor can it allay the problems of an upside-down population pyramid— a hastening demographic crisis that I don't have time to properly litigate—but if the British, European, American or Japanese appetite aims to lower it, and jobs are rudely considered unfit, then who is supposed to carry out the necessary professions many are increasingly reluctant, or unable, to fulfil? We can attempt the imaginative act of convincing Brits that such work is indeed worthy of their higher education and will come with fair pay (unlikely), or we can continue exploiting migrant labour. Or do we fancifully believe we can rapidly automate every menial job, while imagining that doing so would be fine and without greater worry, and do so with more unemployed who may be morosely thankful for newly-invented artificial jobs or pre-served via generous welfare? What are we choosing? This broader issue (regarding work and who does it, the quality of work and its future, etc.) is a se-rious question for which we don't have a durable answer, and the role of the university is part of the equation. Is it really sustainable as well as socially robust to suggest all aspiring British children go to university? We want to preserve the integrity and vital role of the university without it being a place of elite-only admittance unavailable to the lower classes. Yet if we cannot figure out a reworking of what qualifications are required for a good career, re-duce the widening inequality of pay (which only en-ervates economic performance and social cohesion), let alone mitigate our broader demographic and eco-logical challenges, then a scale of such far-ranging and immense problems does not bode well for the health and future of our institutions. If demography trends in its current direction, we may not have the option of an overabundance of new students to send to university anyway . . .

We aren't choosing, we have no real strategy, and we aren't particularly aware of any consequences. The current course favours more and more students unsustainably going to university in a precarious job market, with all of the above mentioned exploitations and grievances intact. We will keep up our pretensions and continue struggling with housing, equality, work, immigration, and more without much consideration of what to do to alleviate our disorder, with no workable or coherent plan beyond demagoguery and fraud promising relief from a crisis after which we can only expect more abuse. We will not build a new order. Rather, we will make a crack in the edifice of the old one where uncertain and volatile impulses fester, and where poor results are more predictable than anything good.

Spring 2025

LANGUAGE AND MORAL PROGRESS

HERE is a type of violence done to language, a sort that should not presume stuffy prescriptivism and definitive declarations on the proper use of words as a response to mend it. The open and euphemistically flexible manner of language's evolution today, with great creativity in colloquial spaces that quicker than ever lurches into popular acceptance, still manages to portray the gall and arrogance of an official decree. Whether haughtily professional, or slick and popular, words are made *essential*, and however clunky and barren, they must be obeyed.

A technocratic and bureaucratic stink wafts over language. The frightening success of *populism* comes with a rejection of this perceived, stifling arrogance, making official language conform more with the *improper*, less inhuman customs of personal talk than with the sacralised, formulaic vocabulary of official institutions. Older types of despotism tried to make the fluid language of the private sphere conform with fixed terms of the state. Now we have a reverse situation, and it is no less distressing. While the standards of authoritarian populist communication are closer to unprofessional *regular speech* than to technocracies, they are still deeply vulgar and encourage deranged thinking and intolerance; appearing worldly, occasionally touching a real grievance, while killing the real world with nonsense and cultish superstition. The language of the state should maintain a respectable professionalism—not too distant and alienating, and not so crude and undignified. We don't want to abandon good standards or be so unpleasant, sacrificing the integrity of constitutions and institutions, yet the resentful animus of authoritarian demagogues holds greater power than the far less destructive alternatives. They unfortunately *are* the future, with their legions of support with real plans of action, whether they are cynical entrepreneurs or sincere violators of truth. The technocratic language of centrism has become, in the hearts of many, deeply untrustworthy. People don't wish to be fooled, yet this impulse suffers from self-betrayal. Those seeking to avoid the distrustful appearance of previous maligned regimes fall foul, deceived, yet not unsurprisingly, into the designs of the most dishonourable actors, the *populists* of the right, despots who the less devious among us have no good strategy for outwitting.

I've noted sociological reasons for this before: the crisis of trust and worsening conditions, bad times creating worse. Yet there is another dimension in the world of language and how we are told to use it.

Language that does not flow, that feels clunky, ugly, *corporate*, that appears imposed from above as if devised by a committee, strikes us as inorganic and undemocratic. Words we use for the presentation of good and justified causes become stale, flat, ridden with potted-phrases, worn out clichés, and this really does do us *and* fair ideas a disservice. Rather than feeling creative and organic, an overbearing professionalism of sterile vocabulary insults beauty and familiarity.

A culture that is too scientistic, literal-minded and *instrumental* may too forsake aesthetics and beauty. *Eminent merits* lose something and can appear artificial and affected instead of spontaneous and natural. Good causes, the most important moral and political matters, not only have the influence of clinical linguistic essentialism but an intolerance for the everyday, permanently imperfect use of language, scolding the innocent misapplication of a name and sowing division. One would struggle to pay for better sabotage. Self-sabotage is free. Rather than creating solidarity and real collective action, good strategy, with a workable order of how to proceed, we are met with a vulgar face haughtily berating us for imperfection—we don't get a productive, or constructive method. Moralisers, either tepid centrists or on the further reaches of the left, speak with a facsimile of political language, using all the latest political jargon, but whether or not they are morally justified and true they are still too often operating outside of *real politics*. It is possible to speak using all the correct and popular political language while still being depoliticised. Some of that language is indeed stifling and unconstructive, and renders us apathetic, confused, or unable to do anything. Anger, righteous fury and hurt are comprehensible drives, but efficacy and utility are worth more. A political or general moral idea is not bad just because a nasty person supports it, just as recoiling from a worthy cause because so many proponents of worthy causes are inferior people is as absurd as refusing to travel by train because you dislike the ticket-collector's face, to misquote Orwell. Yet the practical results of inferior people or dislikable faces are hard to deny. Too many really do refuse to board the train—and with deep resentment to boot—and unfortunately not just due to poor language. This excuse can only go so far, lest we stray into some form of *victim blaming* and give pernicious reactionaries a free pass, but we should still at least take notice. Orwell also spoke of a need for *intelligent propaganda*, meaning with less philosophically or mechanically alienating talk and with more that ordinary people could find desirable. This reasoning has been neglected, and here I am repeating myself: *substance* is never enough. One needs better circumstances too. Bad form is a gift to one's opponents.

The creativity of language is but a small thing to be revived and enlivened for us to maintain hope.

Spring 2025

COMPROMISED

E ARE eternally compromised. There is a diffuse idea that the past had in its favour a stronger sense of metaphysical or spiritual justification, yet attempts to return to this glorified past are doomed to failure. The present, or the future, offers little consolation or any fine answer to the dreadful questions, where even if an assessment of the world is reasonable and *true* it is spiritually or emotionally unfulfilling—yet the past metaphysical satisfactions are false and cannot be accepted without neglect or self-deception. Anti-Enlightenment thinking comes in many flavours—Christian, non-Christian and anti-Christian, and there is an argument to be said that the totalitarianisms of the 20th century, available thanks to technological innovation, were only pos-

sible with the Enlightenment—as an aberrant misuse or an unfortunate byproduct. Any idea can become degenerate and terrible. Good ideas are easily twisted. Most terrible ideas aren't wholly irrational; they leverage some banal truths to enact
their greater superstitions and barbarism. The Enlightenment is a caricature, and not a pure image of
irreligious reason and logic. It was, variably, Christian and, partly, Kantian. The sure past created the
unsure future, if we're crude. The more pertinent
point is that anyone who would want to reject the
modern world, its produce or its legacy, is in an incapable position, trying to access an unavailable concept. We can't. Pandora's Box is open. A pessimistic
idea is that the post-Enlightenment world of apparent reason and empiricism, in all its multifarious
flavours and with all it has birthed, has disposed of
a past comfort, which is now irretrievable if one values truth. If we want to recover this fulfilment we
either resurrect dead and debunked ideologies or lie
to ourselves in other ways, with sophistry or *woo*. I
find the future daunting and spiritually bereft, with
nature lost, community broken, meaner, more distant, less human. But the past is dead. Surely we
don't have to rely on the past to live fulfilled lives?
Maybe. But I have a troubling image. I don't trust

our capacity, intellectual or emotional, to find anything lost or make a new home that isn't somehow uncomfortable or untrue—there is no answer, only unease. I'm reminded of Werner Herzog's denouncing of psychoanalysis, which is wrong about the details of psychoanalysis (which, charitably, are alien to Herzog), but correct nonetheless in a fundamental way, that Nietzsche or Bernard Williams or H. P. Lovecraft all articulated: too much *reflection* causes an issue. "If you harshly light every last corner of a house, the house will be uninhabitable. It's like that with your soul..." What's significant here is that Herzog isn't really refuting that reflection *works*, that the lights in the rooms won't be lit, or saying those who bring light are fraudulent. They'll succeed. Rather, that the process of doing so is disenchanting, and we can't exactly turn off the lights again and forget what we saw.

With all this worry there is still room for robust moral philosophy, so my anxiety isn't in that realm—as if too much discovery will render us ethically incapable. The best ethical concepts, the ones we need, survive whether there is religion or an afterlife or none, and if ethics is contingent on an afterlife then it is weak. Good ethics exist besides and outside religion or haughty metaphysics, and religious people need ethics that can survive the death of God just as much as nonbelievers. The above is a worry whether one accepts God or not. My inconvenience is instead about *investigating* life so much that we are left even more unsure, or overexposed, with less contentment, little satisfactoriness or fulfilment, where we can never have satisfying replies to life or have engaged in so much studious pondering that we disappoint ourselves, voyaging far away from our placid island. Creative people may have good evasions of this. Plenty of them don't appear to care, and the distractions of art can save them. That, or the fundamental unknown is embraced and made useful.

There are virtues in the past, but they are little use if they are hankerings. Forgetting one's past is to die in some way, yet dwelling over the past is also another death. Is it possible to remember the past while pretending it is not there, or know that Pandora's Box is open, the lights are all on, yet pretend we still live in darkness? Better people than me might have a go.

Summer 2025

CREATIVITY

ECENTLY, at least since the beginning of this year (2025), I've been getting carried away or distracted by daydreams of writing short articles. I enjoy writing these brief essays between one thousand and four thousand words, sometimes with an acute point but with room to meander and be personal. I risk writing rambling diary entries instead of remaining focused, which puts what I write beneath serious study. I enjoy the medium of short essays because I think a writer is better, at least for me, as a talented aphorist, with brevity as the soul of wit, instead of writing ponderously and with too many miles of words to cover. I try to impart something that's not so hard to comprehend, but I'm still vain enough to make things flowery and verbose.

Much of my past writing has lingered on illness and my fragile mortality, but that becomes a little too overbearing for my senses after a while. Somehow, political philosophy and historical epistemology are more relieving. There is an easy criticism of course that I'm mostly parroting others I believe to be well-informed or insightful, and in much of those essays I am anticipating, while not explicitly mentioning, particular political and moral actors who I take issue with and who would surely take issue with me. My intentions and what I commend or dislike are hopefully clear enough. I know what names and pejoratives are available to me. I'm no professional and, once more, it concerns me little whether what I say has already been said by another. Most writing is secondhand in some way, I am always in debt to others. I am fine with criticism as long as it is not rude, manipulative, vapid sloganeering or unduly personal. This is difficult for many who make a habit of mean criticism, but the equivocal commitment I have to such ideas should mean I'm not politically ossified, while hopefully also not a pushover. I can take productive criticism. And I can still admire personally disagreeable thinkers, pilfering their stock while not accepting the whole deal. Were I not to write the repetitive motifs in my brief essays, such thoughts would remain lodged in my head, and their lack of release would be aggravating. I value their expression in shorter forms as I don't have the fortitude for a large and comprehensive tract or prolonged thesis.

Yet it is also because I am lazy, or more sympathetically, I lack the energy, time, and mental strength to maintain attention in large tomes — and I am quickly exhausted in most mentally or physically demanding tasks. I take Montaigne's advice: it is okay to admit forgetfulness, weakness, and while scholarship is worthy, there is little need for most to persist in reading anything they really dislike. Dislikable ideas can still be honestly reviewed without making oneself ill. Montaigne was more well-read than any of us even in the 16th-century, and he still thought it fine to drop any book on a whim or for petty reasons. Health and happiness comes before any duty to read large books. My time is precious and I value not wasting it more than needed on tedious prolixity. I leave that to others.

I have been thinking a lot about my admiration for creative people (mostly painters and writers) with my parochial distance from 'creative centres'. This is a distance that's doubled not just geographically but by illness and circumstance, thus preventing my participation in interacting so eas- ily with creative people. I then admire their abil- ity from afar, most of the time, and gain a brief enchantment from my otherwise *ontologically flat- tened* world when I can personally interact with cre- ative, writerly people. I become depressed: my im- mediate surroundings are not populated by people I can talk with fluidly and at length about things I care for. I can talk *at* people who briefly tolerate my presence and know my eager, lonely desperation to want to ramble on about the day's events or the max- ims of La Rochefoucauld, but they don't genuinely know or care about these things as I do. This is no reason to resent them. People have busy lives, and I don't begrudge their difference. I can still note the difference and reasonably desire other forms of com- munity. Common conversation involves furniture and idle talk about new traffic signals more than anything *substantive*, and substantive talk doesn't have to be politically overwhelming. I think the fear of politics, the confusion, and wish to absent our- selves from having to think about it at all, with it being so exhausting, further depoliticises us and makes not just narrowly political conversation, but broader conversation about art and any vaguely sig- nificant, non-trivial subject uncomfortable. Serious but non-political conversation becomes too difficult as well. We are overwhelmed by regular images of tragedy, which makes us sociopathic or apathetic. What is possible if the world is unbearable? I don't wish to be an irritating nerd speaking of atoms and the universe over small talk: those sorts are equally frustrating—it is also important to know when to shut up. It is worth knowing when to avoid talk where one isn't prepared or strong enough. It is instead the case that few I know in my regular personal life are great at the art of conversation, and neither am I, while versatile conversation can be compared to swimming. Small talk and idle chatter serve a purpose, but this is the ability to stay afloat or simply not sink. More meaningful conversation about the wider world, or self-reflection, means diving under the waves. But the neurotic nerd who starts a conversation with facts about the planet Saturn or Rohingya genocide statistics is someone who has sunk and cannot come up for air. Artful conversation means being able to swim well in all the watery conditions of human speech, and I am more prone to sinking than floating, yet I am stuck with a limited ability to swim very well (are the water metaphors too much?) and feel like a dead, drifting fish.

We suppose that technology and mass communication should help? And yet . . .

I read a review by Michele Pridmore-Brown in the *Times Literary Supplement* about John Calhoun's famous experiments with mice and their apparent applications to human sociology. In these artificial conditions, mice developed that were sterile losers lost to inaction and the brute effects of their poor social conditions, sanctimoniously named 'beautiful ones'. Many humans seemingly resemble 'beautiful ones', lost and cut adrift, sexless dead ends, and Calhoun was prescient about the internet as a possible method for solving the problems of socialisation. Meanwhile, never mind the lack of evidence for the 'behavioural sink' of Calhoun's experiments in nature without artificial intervention, "the most salient examples of human pathological sinks, ironically, now occur in virtual hyper-connected spaces that, in Calhoun's view, were supposed to deliver us from our Darwinian selves."

My lack of regular socialisation is not solved by the internet. One can meet fine people and find entertainment but I look at the digital landscape and feel a dissatisfied twinge of disgust and sadness. I want an ideal image—meeting people as fleshy agents in artistic expression. Online forums feel aloof or uncomfortable, insensitive, cold, and unfulfilling more than they might be otherwise. Or least this is my grumpy (or self-righteous) experience in surveying these spaces. They lack the feeling of being tactile or acting out-and-about in the world, as if I were removed from real interactions and must make do with inferior digital substitutes. If I were more pretentious I'd bring up *The Matrix* . . .

Someone else will have an easier solution to this. They can join clubs and recreational spaces with the likeminded. For me, this is physically demanding, and I selfishly wish art would come to me rather than I go to it. I don't want to be relieved of my parochial experience, if that's possible, by having to abscond to oppressive cities or out of my way each time. But the centre won't expand on my whim, so if left to my own devices I'm alone and neglected. People don't have a duty to care about my selfish wants, though I still feel trapped and aloof like some animal in human skin.

Some have the strength to be alone and maintain a fair level of comfort. Most don't. We greatly undervalue friendship, too often seeing it as something secondary or inferior to romance or family. Yet the best life is likely impossible without friendship—a subtler kind of love we fail to describe as glowingly as others, when it no doubt deserves it. I hopelessly want to cultivate more friends, but my fundamental awkwardness prevents any smooth engagement. For all my verbosity it still eludes and confounds me.

Beyond all these worries, with problems beyond my limited abilities, the above dire predictions for the world make creativity more precious. I regard what I say not just as criticism or theory but a creative and indulgent testimony. Setting it down and deliberating over words is an artistic choice as well as a utilitarian one. I could choose other media to get across my thoughts, write more palatable journalism, deeper scholarship, or find some other medium . . . yet for too many reasons this is less opportune to me. Writing is still the most efficient way for me to convey heavy ideas. Film can produce immediate emotion, but one cannot derive the complex inner world of a literary corpus in a motion picture, or a painting—while they are beautiful and better at what writing cannot do.

Creativity and the love of words, books, turns of phrase that make you stand out of your seat, give me some reprieve from what else afflicts me. Life is less artful without the effort to selfishly write down our beliefs and fears, figuring out what one thinks about others, augmenting the light of the world with a reminder or a reiteration. I don't have the stamina to be too extensive, nor do I have the strength to give it up for a quiet life of zen. Bad writing still serves a purpose, whether we can laugh at it or because it may reveal a path towards wisdom through mistakes.

I take relief in many entertainments, lowly or lofty, but even after neglect, it is books, articles, essays, and affirmations of one's ideas and existence that give me the most assurance, and heeding those assurances from others—even when deeply unsure, or unresolved and weary—moves me onward.

> "There is no man, however wise," he said to me, "who has not, at some time in his youth, said things, or even led a life, of which his memory is disagreeable and which he would wish to be abolished. But he absolutely should not regret it, because he can't be assured of becoming a sage—to the extent that that is possible—without having passed through all the ridiculous or odious incarnations that must precede that final incarnation."
>
> —Marcel Proust (Elstir's advice to Marcel), *À l'ombre des jeunes filles en fleurs*

Creativity delivers me, temporarily, from the discomfort of being alone. The loneliness of writing and illness is less stressful if it is shared, or simply expressed, even without any expectation of impact or material effect on the world. I choose to be equivocal more often than clearly declarative, to honestly reflect my own doubts and a humility more in-demand commentators should show, however uncomfortable or unpopular this makes them. Expertise itself becomes tainted when it strays too far, when it fails to interrogate itself, fails to defer to others, and gives us less reason to find others trustworthy. Overconfidence appears necessary despite its dishonesty, and fraudsters thrive more than our better artists. I yearn to say things aloud and not keep everything to myself, but I can't comfortably expect a guarantee or be satisfied. I can live with low expectations when higher ones aren't fair. Our merit should be measured by virtue more than fortune. I have written for myself as my subject regardless of any notice. That is enough.

Spring 2025

Jake Goldsmith is a writer with cystic fibrosis and the founder of The Barbellion Prize, a book prize for ill and disabled authors. He is the author of *Neither Weak Nor Obtuse* (2022) and *In Hospital Environments* (2024) and is a contributing editor to *Exacting Clam*.